W9-AXT-095

The Hamptons Diet

Also by Fred Pescatore, M.D.

Feed Your Kids Well

Thin For Good

The Allergy and Asthma Cure

The Hamptons Diet

Lose Weight Quickly and Safely with
the Doctor's Delicious Meal Plans

FRED PESCATORE, M.D.

WILEY

John Wiley & Sons, Inc.

Copyright © 2004 by Fred Pescatore. All rights reserved

Published by John Wiley & Sons, Inc., Hoboken, New Jersey
Published simultaneously in Canada

Design and production by Navta Associates, Inc.

No part of this publication may be reproduced, stored in a retrieval system, or transmitted in any form or by any means, electronic, mechanical, photocopying, recording, scanning, or otherwise, except as permitted under Section 107 or 108 of the 1976 United States Copyright Act, without either the prior written permission of the Publisher, or authorization through payment of the appropriate per-copy fee to the Copyright Clearance Center, 222 Rosewood Drive, Danvers, MA 01923, (978) 750-8400, fax (978) 646-8600, or on the web at www.copyright.com. Requests to the Publisher for permission should be addressed to the Permissions Department, John Wiley & Sons, Inc., 111 River Street, Hoboken, NJ 07030, (201) 748-6011, fax (201) 748-6008.

The information contained in this book is not intended to serve as a replacement for the advice of a physician. Any use of the information set forth in this book is at the reader's discretion. The author and publisher specifically disclaim any and all liability arising directly or indirectly from the use or application of any information contained in this book. A health care professional should be consulted prior to following any new diet.

For general information about our other products and services, please contact our Customer Care Department within the United States at (800) 762-2974, outside the United States at (317) 572-3993 or fax (317) 572-4002.

Wiley also publishes its books in a variety of electronic formats. Some content that appears in print may not be available in electronic books. For more information about Wiley products, visit our web site at www.wiley.com.

ISBN 0-471-47812-1

Printed in the United States of America

10 9 8 7 6 5 4 3

This book is dedicated to SHF, completely and forever

AUTHOR'S NOTE

The information in this book reflects the author's own experience and is not intended to replace the advice of your personal physician. It is not the intent of the author to diagnose illness or prescribe treatment. The intent is only to help you lose weight and become healthier, using methods that have worked for my patients. Only your personal physician can determine whether this program is suitable for you, depending on your medical history. Your physician should be aware of all your medical conditions and any medications or nutritional supplements you may be taking. This book is not meant to serve as a replacement for your personal physician. If you are on diuretics or diabetes medications, you should proceed only under a doctor's supervision. In addition to having regular checkups and supervision, you should discuss any questions or symptoms that may arise with your personal physician.

In the event that you use the information in this book without your doctor's approval, you are prescribing for yourself, and we assume no responsibility. As with any plan, the weight loss phases of this nutritional program should not be used by patients on dialysis or by pregnant or nursing women.

CONTENTS

ACKNOWLEDGMENTS

I could not have written this book without the kind and generous support of all my patients throughout the years. The fact that they trust me with their lives and the lives of their loved ones is a true testament to their courage and their faith in the healing process. I could never do what I do without their encouragement and understanding. Thank you.

I also wish to thank MW, DC, LL, AR, MI, AH, DR, TV, EM, and, of course, TM. They assist me in so many ways that I can't mention in such a small space. You guys mean a lot to me, although I don't always get the chance to tell you. Thanks.

CHAPTER 1

What Is the Hamptons Diet?

The Hamptons are a forty-mile stretch of land on the southern shore of Long Island in New York State. First settled in the mid-1600s, the area boasts 300-year-old trees, hundreds of acres of farmland, gorgeous dunes, sea cliffs, and stunning beaches. The Hamptons didn't really "arrive" until the late 1800s, when the railroad was built from New York City. From that era up to the present, the eastern end of Long Island has been synonymous with the good life: sun, fun, glamour, and lots of money.

The "country"—as some of us city dwellers call the Hamptons— is one of the most beautiful places on the planet. It is a place where you can leave your doors unlocked, know everyone by his or her first name, can see the stars at night in all their glory while hearing the ocean's roar, yet can still have a great meal. The houses are picture-postcard perfect, the gardens are lush and inviting, and the oceanfront and the beaches have been voted among the best in the world.

Each season has its own special allure. Autumn brings dazzling colors as far as the eye can see. Spring blossoms with an amazing array of gorgeous flowers wherever you turn. Even in the winter, the towns have an unsurpassed charm. Small, tasteful, beautifully lit trees line every Main Street for the holidays, and some Christmas trees even seem to float in ponds.

I have a summer home in East Hampton, and the Hamptons Diet was formulated with the belief that millions of people want to be thin, rich, and famous—like many of my clientele. Since most of us will never be any of those things, this book will show you how to accomplish two out of these three goals: You can be rich in the one area that counts—monounsaturated-rich (I'll explain later)—and thin, by following this well-tested diet, used by many of my Hamptons clients. The Hamptons Diet will help you lose weight and achieve a healthier lifestyle.

This book differs from my first adult diet book, *Thin For Good,* because this one really gets down to basics. *Thin For Good* explored much of the science behind insulin resistance, metabolic syndrome (Syndrome X), and diabetes. *The Hamptons Diet* provides the simple tools you'll need to get healthy by eating more nutritious foods. The diets in both books are a modified low-carbohydrate approach, but the Hamptons Diet is more streamlined. This book draws on the wealth of knowledge I've gained from treating many more patients since *Thin For Good* was released. *The Hamptons Diet* also draws on scientific discoveries that have been made since then. Now you can embark on the most current and up-to-date low-carb diet available, while taking advantage of the newest technology—the health benefits of monounsaturated fats.

Ooooh, how rich and sinful! That's the most common expression I hear when I explain to newcomers the basis of the Hamptons Diet. They can't believe that they will lose weight while being so indulgent. Well, that is the basis of the Hamptons themselves—indulge yourself and be fabulous because of it. If you have ever been to the Hamptons, the first thing you will notice is that the place is not about depriving yourself, but rather is about indulgence. It wasn't always that way; the Hamptons are rooted in old Yankee traditions, more New England than glitzy New York. But, like everything else, the Hamptons have changed with the times and always stay one step ahead. Now I'm giving away the secrets of the stars so we can all be thin and healthy.

In *Thin For Good,* I brought the Atkins philosophy to a new level by teaching people that they could eat healthy complex carbohydrates while maintaining a low-carbohydrate lifestyle. *The Hamptons Diet* goes even further, by showing the dramatic changes that you can make in your life by simply eating healthful oils.

Fat Is Not a Bad Word

The first meaning of the word *fat* that I can recall was that it meant *me*. That's how I identified myself. I was a fat kid—no getting around that. I was the largest boy in my class. Fat was simply descriptive of who I was. Everyone in my life was fat: both of my parents, my siblings, and most of my extended family. Being fat was normal, so the word wasn't really a problem for me.

Food held a *very* prominent role in my life. Every meal was an extravaganza. During this time, I learned that a single serving of ice cream was a pint. Not until college did I find out that other families do not start each meal with a pasta course. I was shocked to discover that pasta, in and of itself, could be a meal.

This was also when I began to understand the power that food could have. Food could comfort you, be your best friend, take the edge off a bad day, go to the movies with you, and just plain be an activity all unto itself. Food was my favorite companion: While watching TV, I'd eat; if listening to the radio, I'd eat; when lying by the pool or on the beach, I'd eat; while reading a book or doing homework, I'd eat. I used to plan activities around which foods I could eat by taking part in that activity. I associated events with food. Going to the ballpark meant hot dogs; going to Little League meant ice cream. I participated simply for the food. It's no wonder people constantly made fun of me for being fat.

After several years, I began to examine an alternative lifestyle— being thin. But I didn't know where to begin. Eventually, I succeeded by using a diet plan that's very similar to the one you'll read about in this book.

In 1994, I joined the practice of Robert Atkins, the late famous diet doctor, and fat became my friend. He touted the message of "Eat all the fat you want. Fat will set you free. Fat doesn't give you cholesterol, sugar does. Eat fat and get thin"—what a perfect message for an overweight person. That experience was mind-opening. I witnessed thousands of people losing weight and getting healthy, yet modern science told me that everything he said was wrong and scandalous. Keep in mind that I started working with him before his work was vindicated and before his work was back on the best-seller list. This was all new to me.

As a scientist, I wanted to know more. I wanted to know where Dr. Atkins's beliefs came from and why this plan worked. This led me to my present quest. The study of fats and oil is fascinating and wrought with intrigue, drama, politics, backstabbing, and science. It's one great big scientific epic soap opera.

For now, the evidence clearly points to the proper fats one should eat. With up to 40 percent of all Americans choosing to watch their intake of carbohydrates, their diets will subsequently be higher in fats. People need to receive a clear message about which fats to eat and which to avoid. That message has been very understated until now. Since we all agree that there are healthful fats, which ones are they?

As the former associate medical director of the Atkins Center in New York City, the "all-fat-is-good-for-you" message was the main thing that Bob Atkins and I disagreed on. In *Thin For Good,* I differentiated my diet message from his. In this book, I will focus much more attention on the health benefits of some fats and the need to avoid certain other fats. This is information that my audiences have clamored for.

The Hamptons Diet will teach you how to lose weight, get healthy, and eat really well in the process. The diet will work to ameliorate the problems of insulin resistance, Syndrome X, diabetes, cardiovascular disease, cancer risk, allergies, and asthma. The Hamptons Diet is a breakthrough method to decrease inflammation, decrease health risk, enhance energy, and prolong life. You will learn how to diet by learning about fat.

I told you my story because I wanted to write this book not as a doctor but as someone who is out there in the trenches with you—trying to sort everything out and make sense of all the confusing nutritional data that abounds in our society, and stay thin, too.

The one diet that has been significantly studied—and which I have modified in *The Hamptons Diet*—is the Mediterranean diet. This diet, in particular, has been vindicated in many recent studies as the healthiest way to eat. By eating this way, you can lower your risk of heart disease, diabetes, and arthritis and live longer in the process.

The basic premise of the Hamptons Diet is to eat more vegetables, fish, and omega-3 fatty acids and to consume most of your fats in the form of monounsaturates, a premise shared by the Mediterranean diet. The primary monounsaturated fat that is used in the Mediterranean diet is olive oil. Modern science now knows of an oil that has even more monounsaturated fat than olive oil, up to 30 percent more monounsaturates: macadamia nut oil. *The Hamptons Diet* updates this important dietary concept of Mediterranean eating by enhancing the most significant part of the program, making it more monounsaturated-rich by using macadamia nut oil. The Hamptons Diet contains some of the most up-to-date science available. A study published in the *American Journal of Clinical Nutrition* in February 2004 by Dr. Christine Pelkman reported that moderate-fat diets rich in monounsaturated fats were better at reducing weight and lowering risk for cardiovascular disease, and they were easier to follow.

This book will reveal the wonders of macadamia nut oil, one of the highest food sources of monounsaturated fats in the world. You'll learn why it is sanctioned by the Australian Heart Association and given to cardiac patients for its health benefits. Macadamia nut oil is one of the best features of this diet program. If macadamia nut oil is not available in your area, check the resource section of this book. In my opinion, the finest macadamia nut oil is imported from Australia. If you don't like macadamia nut oil—not that I've ever known anyone who doesn't—or if you're allergic to nuts, then an estate-bottled extra virgin olive oil is the second-best oil to use on this diet program.

The Hamptons Diet includes all the health benefits that come from eating lean meats, fish, vegetables, and fruits, coupled with the richest source of monounsaturated fat, macadamia nut oil. I think this is the healthiest diet program currently available. In this book, you'll learn how I improved on the USDA food pyramid by devising the Hamptons Diet Pyramids.

Can you face a life without bread, pasta, ice cream, and all the good stuff? Everyone who tries a low-carb diet faces this question. Brady, a twenty-eight-year-old father of two, asked me the same thing. He is a trader on Wall Street and is used to the perks that come along with that position—fancy clothes, fancy beach houses, and lots of wining and dining. He had only about twenty pounds to lose. His real reason for seeing me was that his stomach really bothered him. He had constant gas and a bloated feeling throughout the day, which became worse after he ate anything. He also had an urgent need to move his bowels immediately after each meal. He experienced acid reflux and was taking a little purple pill that he really didn't want to take. He had been diagnosed with irritable bowel syndrome.

After ensuring that he had no real serious gastrointestinal issues, I outlined his monounsaturated-rich diet program, which was designed to eliminate his need for any reflux medication and to correct his bowel disturbances. I explained that he was experiencing so many of those symptoms due to an imbalance in his digestive tract—the underlying cause was inflammation. To correct that, he needed a diet that specifically eliminated inflammation. Since monounsaturated fats do this, the Hamptons Diet was for him.

Although he'd never been on a diet in his life, he stuck to the tenets of this one completely and was a model patient. He lost twenty pounds, went from a size 36 waist to a 32, and, after the first week or so, never had any other bowel problems or acid reflux. It has now been three years since he first started his monounsaturated-rich lifestyle. Brady admitted that since he was a novice dieter, he was a little confused at first, but after the first two weeks, he had all the tenets in place and found the diet easy to follow. Brady did it, and he was so impressed with his success that he referred everyone he knew to me—the clearest indicator of how successful a diet is.

The Hamptons Diet is for you, if

- You want to lose weight and get healthy.
- You want to drop dress sizes or pants sizes.
- You want to feel great.
- You believe in low-carbohydrate dieting but don't want to give up all carbohydrates and want to eat only the healthiest fats.
- You want to eat really well, since eating well is the best revenge.
- You want to be monounsaturated-rich.
- You are over the age of twelve—anyone younger should be following the diet outlined in my first book, *Feed Your Kids Well.*

The Hamptons Diet provides you with guidelines that will help you make healthy eating choices. The diet is a modified low-carb approach that also teaches you how to eat *healthy* carbohydrates without gaining weight. It allows you to eat fat but not all the fat you can eat and only the *healthiest* fats.

So, let fat back into your life and into your kitchen. Let's try to make this word have a really good meaning: fat = thin = happy = healthy = longer life. Enjoy the book. Eat good fats. Embrace the Hamptons lifestyle, even if you have never been to the beach or live far away from the ocean. Get thin and healthy in the process—you can lose up to fourteen pounds in just two weeks! Most important, have fun.

CHAPTER 2

The Hamptons Diet and Your Health

Carolyn was an interesting patient. She was in her early forties and at least fifty pounds overweight. She had been a child actress but never again achieved the success she had in her teens. This contributed to the emotional baggage she lugged around in regard to her weight issues. Yet now she wanted to revive her career, had an opportunity to star in a talk show, and didn't want to play the role of an aged housewife any longer. She knew she had to start with her weight.

The other day in the office, I had an amazing revelation. I looked around and noticed that all of my patients were women. Then I realized that this very often was the case. At that moment, a light bulb went off in my head: Women are supposedly healthier than men, and they have longer life expectancies. No one really knows what to attribute this to, but it came to me that the reason women live longer is that they utilize the health-care system more than men do. Perhaps they get better taken care of not because they take better care of themselves, as is often theorized, but because they allow someone to take care of them. It's just a thought, but one I want to share with the guys out there in my audience.

Besides being overweight, Carolyn also had high cholesterol, mild hypertension, and elevated triglyceride levels in her blood. After getting her blood tests back from the lab, I diagnosed her with Syndrome X or metabolic syndrome—a common disease that affects about 70 million Americans. Fortunately, more physicians are beginning to understand the devastating impact of this combination of metabolic factors that leads to high incidences of heart disease and stroke, and some are even learning how to correct this condition.

Since even modern science can't dispute that a low-carbohydrate diet would be appropriate to treat her condition, I started her on the "A" diet program, which I will outline for you shortly. In three months, all of her cardiac risk parameters had dramatically improved: Cholesterol dropped from 287 to 176; triglycerides from 335 to 56; homocysteine from 13.4 to 8.7; and C-reactive protein from 3.4 to 1.0. She also lost forty pounds in those three months, and her blood pressure returned to normal. She happily remarked that it was too easy—she should have had to suffer to get such dramatic results. No one has to suffer on the Hamptons Diet to achieve success. All anyone needs to do is follow the simple steps.

Carolyn's experience illustrates the tremendous benefits of combining a low-carbohydrate diet with a focus on monounsaturated–fat(s). Not only will you lose weight, you'll be healthier. One way that the Hamptons Diet accomplishes this is by lowering inflammation in the internal environment of your body through good, sound, scientific, and well-researched nutrition. We are about to embark on a nutritional journey that will show you exactly how to balance the omega-3 and omega-6 fatty acids in your diet—the key to controlling inflammation. By using beneficial monounsaturated fats and cutting out sugar and simple carbohydrates, you will feel great and lose weight.

Are You Still on the Fence?

Many people still can't accept the fact that not all fats are unhealthful. Perhaps no one ever taught you the benefits of fat or showed you the type of fat that you need to eat to be healthy and lower your risk of heart disease, high blood pressure, diabetes, certain cancers, and one of the largest problems today—the metabolic syndrome. A monounsaturated-rich diet can do all of those things. The Hamptons Diet also emphasizes eating whole and real foods as much as possible.

Not too many years ago, no one thought twice about deep frying food or spreading what is now considered "sudden cardiac death"–size amounts of butter on vegetables or toast. Likewise, red meat was considered an essential part of the diet and eating it showed that you had arrived and were able to afford to eat costly meat. However, the twist is that despite these eating habits, fewer Americans were fat then. Sure, there were some overweight people—about 13 to 14 percent of the population, a level that stayed steady during the heady days of the 1960s and 1970s.

During the 1980s, the number of overweight adults increased by 8 percent and by the end of the decade, nearly 1 in 4 Americans was overweight or obese. This steep rise continued through the 1990s to today. For children, the story is worse. During the same period, the number of overweight children tripled.

This epidemic started when the low-fat dogma took off in earnest, when the food pyramid began to be touted as a healthy eating model. People were told and believed: If you don't eat fat, you won't be fat. Fat causes heart disease. Eating cholesterol makes your cholesterol levels rise. These mantras, repeated over and over, were developed in the early 1980s—not very long ago.

In fact, until the 1970s, it was generally accepted that fat and protein protected us from overeating because these foods satisfied the appetite, leaving us less hungry. This belief, held for hundreds of years, was eliminated in the blink of an eye by a government and a food manufacturing industry mutually dependent on each other for revenue. The low-fat dogma basically arose from a myth about fat consumption. Only ambiguous science supports the claims that consuming dietary fat will cause any of the health problems plaguing our population. In the late 1970s, the government released a report advising people to significantly reduce their fat intake to achieve better health, and the food manufacturing industry took advantage of this change by marketing low-fat foods to consumers.

Soon, there was an abundance of foods being hailed as reduced-fat, low-fat, or non-fat. The funniest one is milk. Whole milk is 4 percent fat. Low-fat milk is usually 2 percent. What is the difference?

One of the most troubling aspects of the low-fat message was that people weren't encouraged to eat foods naturally low in fat; instead, we were advised to consume man-made foods, atrocities that should never have been allowed to be called food. When fat is removed from a food, something has to be added for it to have flavor or taste the way we think it should. Sugar, in the form of high fructose corn syrup or some other variation, is the usual substitute. This change in the makeup of processed food caused our per-capita consumption of sugar to rise dramatically. Cheap, over-refined oils and trans-fatty acids also pervade these foods. When you look at a package of low-fat cookies, for example, there is hardly anything that can be considered as real ingredients, not tampered with by man.

The low-fat myth also encouraged unlimited consumption of foods as long as they didn't have any fat. The same is happening now with the low-carb message. Food manufacturing companies are rushing to produce foods that are low in carbohydrates, and these foods are flying off supermarket shelves. However, most of the packaging is misleading; consumers must learn to eat foods naturally low in carbohydrates, not man-made, chemically manipulated foods. If you are eating any low-carb packaged food products, please check the labels carefully and make sure you are eating foods naturally low in carbohydrate that do not contain man-made chemical enhancements.

Eat Real Food

We have gotten so far away from eating healthful, real foods that most of us don't even know what they are. The Hamptons approach is to use real foods as meals and snacks. I discourage the use of all low-carbohydrate snack products, such as protein bars, protein shakes, and other false foods, except in real emergency situations where you have no other choice. Otherwise, leave those low-carb foods for the "C" part of the diet. The reason I do this is twofold:

1. By switching from candy bars, prepackaged junk food, and milk shakes to these new types of food, you aren't really challenging your eating habits and changing your behavior. The habits that need to be changed remain the same. If you want to be thin and eat a diet high in monounsaturated fats, then learning to get through a day without these crutches is paramount.

2. Many of these products have artificial ingredients, too. Let's learn how to eat real, unprocessed foods without chemical additives and unhealthful ingredients. The carbohydrate count on these products may be erroneous or, at the very least, misleading. A carbohydrate is a carbohydrate is a carbohydrate. Total grams count, not net or effective grams. In fact, I am currently working on a committee to standardize labels so there is less consumer confusion.

Balance the Scale

Another important aspect of the Hamptons Diet is trying to eat as organically as possible. Now, I know that this can be expensive—believe me, I know. Even I can't afford to eat organic foods all the time and at every meal. Just try to do it as often as you can. The reason for this all boils down to the fatty-acid content of the food we eat and the inflammatory response this sets up in our bodies. The whole purpose of the Hamptons Diet is to heal our internal environment, to allow for improved weight loss and increased health. Thus, we have to decrease inflammation any way we can.

One way to decrease inflammation and regulate our internal environment is by eating true organic meats and meat products. This includes eggs, cheese, and the meat itself. To balance the omega-6 and the omega-3 fatty acids of our diet, we need to consume foods that have as close to 1:1 ratios as possible. I emphasize organic foods because when animals are fed foods that they shouldn't eat, such as grain for cattle and chickens, and so on, the fatty-acid content of their meat changes. The same holds true for eggs. An organic egg has a perfect omega-6 to omega-3 fatty-acid ratio of 1:1. A commercially raised egg has a ratio of up to 19:1 of the harmful pro-inflammatory omega-6 fats. Scientific reports tell us that the same is true when animal protein is tested for its fatty-acid content. So, a key way that we can decrease our omega-6 fatty-acid intake, and thereby decrease inflammation, is to eat organically.

Omega-3 fatty acids are anti-inflammatory and hence decrease inflammation in the body. Omega-6 fatty acids are pro-inflammatory and thus raise inflammation levels in the body. Since our goal is to decrease inflammation and cleanse our internal environment, we should always balance the fatty acids in our diet.

The Hamptons Diet will help you do this. But it's also important for you to understand why you're doing what you're doing. This way, you'll learn how to make healthful choices on your own. I can't possibly comment on all of the foods that exist, but if you follow the guidelines in this book, you can ensure that your diet stays true to the ideal.

Essential Fatty Acids

This is a good time to address the issue of essential fatty acids. There are a total of eight essential fatty acids, which fall into the two classes of omega-6 and omega-3 fatty acids. Omega-6 fatty acids are most abundant in common vegetable oils, such as corn, safflower, cottonseed, and sunflower oils. The highest concentrations of omega-3 fatty acids are found in seafood, green leafy vegetables, and walnuts.

Our bodies function best when there is a perfect balance between these two types of essential fatty acids—just the way Mother Nature intended it. Yet in many industrialized nations, this ratio has become lopsided, with approximately twenty times more omega-6 fatty acids than omega-3s in the average person's diet. This imbalance has been linked to a long list of serious medical conditions. If you look closely enough, you can see that each of the following diseases can be considered a disease of civilization:

- obesity
- heart disease
- hypertension
- insulin resistance
- osteoarthritis
- diabetes
- asthma

- allergies
- cancer
- stroke
- ADD/ADHD
- depression
- schizophrenia
- Alzheimer's disease

So, if you want to fight disease and be healthy, it's important to consume the proper 1:1 ratio of omega-6 to omega-3 fatty acids, which will send cancer-fighting, heart-healthy messages to your entire body. Once you switch to a monounsaturated-rich diet and follow the Hamptons protocols, you will improve your ratio without having to remember the details of this fatty-acid research. The diet of the Japanese is the closest to this ratio, about 2:1, and they have the longest life expectancy and much less heart disease when compared to every other population on the planet.

Our diet is overloaded with omega-6 fatty acids because of our reliance on grain-based sustenance—breads, cereals, pastas, and cakes—and our minimal intake of vegetables and fruits, along with our use of highly processed and damaged oils that are rich in omega-6 fats. The main reason we're so deficient in omega-3 fatty acids isn't that we don't consume enough fish and vegetables (although this is a significant problem that you should keep in mind when shopping for groceries). It's that our ancestors' natural diet contained many more omega-3 fatty acids than ours does. In fact, it's estimated that we eat only one-tenth the amount of omega-3 fatty acids that we need for good health.

It is easy to see why our diet is substandard. We consume

- More poor-quality, degraded oils that lack nutrients and are high in the unhealthful and unbalanced polyunsaturated fats
- More hydrogenated oils
- Less fish
- Foods that have been radically altered and have more omega-6 fatty acids
- Greater amounts of trans-fatty acids
- Increased amounts of sugar

Since omega-3 fatty acids are an important part of the diet and are anti-inflammatory, the following table shows you where to get them. Most of the animal sources are fish. I recommend 1,500 to 3,000 mg per day of omega-3 fish oils in the form of DHA and EPA. The federal government is now recommending 7 grams of these oils per week or 1 gram per day. It's a good first step for government officials, considering that a few years ago, they didn't believe fish oils had any health benefit.

FOODS HIGH IN OMEGA-3 FATTY ACIDS

Fish—DHA and EPA	Plants—Mostly ALA
Pacific mackerel	flaxseeds
Atlantic herring	butternuts (dried)
albacore tuna	English walnuts
chinook salmon	soybeans (raw)
pink salmon	leeks
sablefish	wheat germ
whitefish	almonds
Atlantic mackerel	pinto beans
Pacific oysters	purslane

To give you a better understanding of what and how much you would have to eat to meet the government recommendations, let alone mine, here is a table listing the amount of omega-3 oils (in grams) per cooked, 4-ounce serving of certain fish. Notice that the most popular fish have less omega-3 fatty acids per serving.

OMEGA-3 OIL CONTENT OF COMMONLY EATEN FISH

Fish	Grams per 4 oz
Pacific herring	2.4
Atlantic herring	2.3
Pacific mackerel	2.1
Atlantic salmon	2.1
sablefish	2.0
canned pink salmon	1.9
whitefish	1.9
Pacific oysters	1.6
Atlantic mackerel	1.4

Fish	Grams per 4 oz
red salmon	1.4
coho salmon	1.2
bluefish	1.1
trout	1.1
eastern oysters	1.0
clams, fresh or canned	0.3
rainbow smelt	1.0
whiting (hake)	1.0
freshwater bass	0.9
blue mussels	0.9
swordfish	0.9
rainbow trout	0.8
white canned tuna	0.8
canned sardines	0.7
flounder or sole	0.6
halibut	0.5
rockfish	0.5
shrimp	0.4
snapper	0.4
sturgeon	0.4
Atlantic perch	0.3
haddock	0.3
light canned tuna	0.3
yellowfin tuna	0.3
Atlantic cod	0.2
catfish	0.1

Sources: Center for Science in Public Interest, U.S. Department of Agriculture, National Academy of Science

It's important to remember the fatty-acid profile of your cooking oils and salad oils too. Throughout this book, I'll discuss the miraculous benefits of macadamia nut oil—an oil you can use for both hot and cold recipes. Macadamia nut oil helps to keep your internal environment healthy because

- It has the perfect ratio of omega-6 to omega-3 fatty acids, 1:1.
- It has the highest concentration of healthful monounsaturated fats, or omega-9 fatty acids.
- Its high smoke point will decrease the risk of trans-fatty acid formation.

Macadamia nut oil is the gold standard for reducing inflammation and restoring the health of our internal environment. This oil has the highest concentration of omega-9 fatty acids (monounsaturated fats), specifically the healthiest one, oleic acid. Both the medical establishment and I agree on this one. The National Cholesterol Education Program and the American Heart Association publications believe that the fat in our diet should consist of 80 percent monounsaturates. If you follow the Hamptons Diet and use premium Australian macadamia nut oil, you will achieve this goal without even trying.

When 175 million Americans suffer from some kind of chronic disease, isn't it time to look at some of the simple things we can do to help restore the critical balance that is so lacking in our diet? The Hamptons Diet, whether you follow it because you want to lose weight, get healthy, or both, will allow you to take full advantage of the latest advances in health and nutrition. Basically, this means getting back to eating natural foods, that have been minimally processed.

These steps are the guiding principles of healthful eating and should be part of everyone's lifestyle program, not just people who follow the Hamptons Diet. By following the simple steps outlined in this book, you'll see how easily you can become healthy and lose weight by making a few key adjustments to your everyday routine. The following guidelines will make your lifestyle more healthful. The guidelines for adhering to the Hamptons Diet and losing weight are far simpler than these.

Hamptons Diet Health Tips for Restoring the Health of Your Internal Environment

1. Balance the ratio of omega-6 to omega-3 fatty acids. Try to get to 1:1, if possible.
2. Eat real food—no processed foods, not even supposedly health-ful ones, unless absolutely necessary.
3. Try to eat as organically as possible.
4. If you're unable to eat organically, try to eat as naturally as pos-sible.
5. Buy organic eggs, if you buy nothing else organic.
6. Use macadamia nut oil, if possible, for your oil needs. In doing so, you will automatically consume up to 80 percent of your fats in the form of the most heart-healthful, omega-9 monounsatu-rates—the proven gold standard of healthfulness. Macadamia nut oil has this ratio naturally.
7. Try to eat only fish that has been caught in the wild, not farm raised, if possible.
8. If you have to eat foods that are not real, then eat foods that have been minimally processed.

CHAPTER 3

Updating the Mediterranean Diet

Brenda, a thirty-four-year-old woman, came to see me because she'd just received bad news from her cardiologist. She was diagnosed with high blood pressure but didn't want to take medication. She also had high cholesterol and high triglycerides and was twenty-five pounds overweight—the classic metabolic syndrome. Her doctor said that if she lost weight, she wouldn't have to take medication. When Brenda asked how she should lose weight, the doctor gave her a blank stare and said, "Don't eat any fat, I guess."

This wasn't very encouraging to Brenda, so she decided to look into the subject on her own. Brenda is a well-known screenwriter of television movies and does a lot of research on the Internet. She has a sedentary job but still has to look good at awards ceremonies. Even in this day and age, a woman's looks are important in getting new jobs in the entertainment industry. She was up for an Academy Award this year and had a few months to get into fighting shape for that walk down the red carpet and the run-in with you-know-who. In her research, she kept coming across the Mediterranean diet, and it seemed like the most promising approach. She liked the idea of a diet that encouraged eating good, whole foods and a minimum of processed foods. Since she ate out most nights and enjoyed a very active social calendar, she needed a diet that would suit her lifestyle and would help her to lose weight and feel better in the process. Upon further investigation, she came across my approach, which seemed to take the Mediterranean diet to the next level. It was even more heart-healthy because it increased the levels of the most healthful fats with the use of macadamia nut oil, instead of the traditional olive oil. She further liked the idea that this oil was sanctioned by the Australian Heart Association and was given to heart patients in that country before they resorted to using potentially dangerous medications to lower their cholesterol. The Hamptons Diet made sense to her, so she came to see me.

After two weeks, Brenda had lost eleven pounds and felt more energetic than she had since she was a teenager. By the end of the first month, her blood pressure readings were consistently normal. After three months, she had lost all twenty-five and an additional ten pounds, she had normal blood pressure readings, and her cholesterol had plummeted to 167, with an HDL (good cholesterol) of 71. Her triglycerides were 34. Brenda had successfully cured herself of the metabolic syndrome by following the Hamptons Diet—a modified Mediterranean approach, with an emphasis on monounsaturated-rich macadamia nut oil as the primary cooking oil. Oh, she didn't win the award, but she was thrilled with all the attention she received at the *Vanity Fair* party afterward.

Acquiring Mediterranean Flair

Who wouldn't want to be Mediterranean? The island of Capri captures all the romance of this lifestyle for me—jet-setters, warm water with blues so blue they're almost unreal, warm days and cool evenings, fresh fish caught from the sea, vegetables grown in perfect soil that has been tended with care for generations, and not an overweight person in sight, yet everyone sitting in cafes laughing, eating, and drinking.

With heart disease being the number-one killer in many countries around the world, the scientific community has recently begun to examine the advice that it dispensed for the last twenty-five years. From a public health perspective, when advice is given to increase the health of a population, yet this advice fails, it can mean only two things—either the advice is incorrect, or the advice wasn't communicated properly and the message was altered. Since the low-fat, low-cholesterol debacle was introduced, the rates of heart disease, obesity, and diabetes have not fallen. So, what went wrong?

The low-fat message has been miscommunicated in that it gave people free rein to eat as many fat-free foods as they wanted. These foods can produce unhealthy levels of blood lipids and increase the risk for gaining weight and developing diabetes, which both increase the risk of coronary heart disease. In fact, since the low-fat message was first touted in the 1980s, obesity and diabetes have become epidemic.

The advice was also wrong. The original low-fat advice was postulated on the simple notion that blood cholesterol, specifically LDL (bad) cholesterol, constituted the entire picture of cardiac risk. This theory overlooked the fact that diet affects cardiovascular health on multiple biological pathways, including triglyceride levels, HDL (good) cholesterol, lipoprotein(a), c-reactive protein, homocysteine levels, blood pressure, and blood sugar excursions. All of these factors are influenced by more than just total dietary fat and the amount of cholesterol you eat.

The Mediterranean Diet

I will spend most of this chapter explaining the scientific merits of a Mediterranean diet. Since the Hamptons Diet is an updated, more healthful offshoot of this approach, the same health benefits—and more—would apply.

The American Heart Association (AHA) diet recommends limiting total dietary fat intake to less than 30 percent, saturated fat to less than 10 percent, and your total cholesterol intake to less than 300 mg/day. Although this diet has been shown to lower total cholesterol, it has failed to lower triglyceride levels, and it actually lowers HDL (good cholesterol) levels. The AHA diet has never consistently shown long-term improvement in any heart disease outcome. Triglyceride levels in many recent studies proved to be a more significant indicator of coronary risk than cholesterol levels were, and the recommended AHA diet fails to address this risk factor. Also, some evidence suggests that coronary heart disease continues to progress in patients who follow the AHA diet.

A Mediterranean diet does not regard all fat as bad. The emphasis in this type of diet is not to limit total fat consumption but to make sensible choices about the type of fat you consume. This is the Hamptons approach, too. Two types of fats are considered healthful: omega-3 fatty acids and monounsaturated omega-9 fats. No limits are put on the consumption of these types of fats. Omega-3 fatty acids are found in fatty fish such as tuna and salmon and, in lesser amounts, in some plant sources such as flaxseeds and walnuts. Monounsaturated fats are found in macadamia nut oil, olive oil, nuts, and avocados. Another thing that the Hamptons Diet and the Mediterranean diet have in common is that they both emphasize eating whole, natural, nutritious foods that are low in trans-fatty acids.

How To: The Hamptons Diet

The six basic tenets of the Mediterranean diet and the Hamptons Diet are:

- Eat fish that's rich in omega-3 fatty acids, and eat other good, lean pure protein sources.
- Eat nuts.
- Exclude trans-fatty acids.
- Eat healthful fats: monounsaturated fats (in the Hamptons Diet, we use the most healthful oil—macadamia nut—and in the pure Mediterranean diet, olive oil is used).
- Consume ample quantities of vegetables and some fruits.
- Consume moderate amounts of alcohol.

The health benefits of following these guidelines were recently reviewed by Harvard researchers. One of these scientists, Walter Willett, examined studies of thousands of people to see if any connections could be made between participants' health and what they were eating. The studies were epidemiological and included people who already had heart disease, as well as those who didn't. Thus the results are both valid and accurate. Let's examine the findings, as they relate to the Hamptons Diet.

Eat Fish

The protective effects of eating fish are most likely related to the cardiovascular benefits of omega-3 fatty acids—especially DHA and

EPA. A high consumption of these fatty acids has been shown to decrease mortality by 30 percent and decrease the risk of sudden cardiac death by 45 percent. The mechanisms by which omega-3s protect us are still unknown, but we have discovered that they lower triglycerides, have an anti-inflammatory function, decrease the risk of clots, and prevent abnormal heart rhythms.

The protective effects of eating fish have to be tempered with the health risks caused by their high mercury level and the unwholesome practices of fish farms. If this were a perfect world and we could eat ocean-caught fish that weren't in danger of depletion, then fish would be an ideal protein source. To avoid this conundrum, stick to eating smaller fish like sardines or consume fish oils in a purified capsule form. Keep in mind that pregnant women, those who are nursing, or those who plan to become pregnant within a year are advised not to eat too much fish because of potentially high levels of mercury and other pollutants. These women are especially advised to stay away from bluefish, striped bass, tilefish, swordfish, king mackerel, tuna steaks, white and golden snapper, and any freshwater fish. Canned tuna should also be limited to five ounces per week. In addition, to get the full health benefit of eating fish, we should not eat them battered and deep fried. Sautéing fish in macadamia nut oil is fine, but deep-fried fish sticks and fast-food fish sandwiches do not fit into this category.

Because of these problems, the Hamptons Diet changes this category to Eat Fish and Other Types of Lean Protein. I request that people also consume trimmed beef, trimmed pork, skinned chicken, and other animal forms of protein, including eggs. Just remember to trim off all the excess fat and to emphasize white meat chicken and turkey.

Eat Nuts

These were a significant part of our ancestors' diet, because they are highly nutritious and were easily gathered. Nuts contain protein, carbohydrates, and fat. They also contain vitamin E, folic acid, potassium, and magnesium and do not contain cholesterol. Placing nuts at the top of the USDA food pyramid was a horrible mistake. The lack of emphasis on nuts was probably due to the United States' not growing large amounts of them. Nuts are low in saturated fats, although 80 percent or more of their weight is fat—but good fat. Most of the fat comes in the form of monounsaturates and omega-3 fatty acids, making nuts an extremely healthful food. Keep in mind that peanuts are not nuts but are legumes, so they're not included in this category of foods. Learn to enjoy other nuts, like macadamia nuts, walnuts, pecans, and hazelnuts. They should be plain or roasted, not honey roasted.

The scientific evidence that nuts prevent coronary heart disease is starting to accumulate. Several large, long-term, population-based studies show that people who ate nuts more than four times per week lowered their risk for heart disease by 50 percent. In women, the lowered risk was 35 percent, when compared with those who rarely ate nuts. Nuts have been shown to decrease total, as well as LDL, cholesterol, and therein lies the probable mechanism for their health benefit. In fact, almonds are now approved to carry a heart-healthy seal, which is a big step in the right direction.

Exclude Trans-Fatty Acids

This is a primary dictate of the Hamptons Diet. Trans-fatty acids are prevalent in many foods because they're cheaper and they increase shelf life longer than any other type of fat. These man-made molecules, produced during the hydrogenation of vegetable oil, are the most dangerous fats in our diet. The largest offender in this category is margarine. Studies show that trans-fatty acids increase the risk of heart disease at least as much as some saturated fats do, and they are implicated in up to 30,000 deaths each year in the United States alone.

Yet the labeling law requiring levels of this fat to be clearly marked on food products doesn't take effect until 2006. This is the most dangerous type of fat, yet the food manufacturing industry continues to lobby over the specifics of what the updated label will say. This critical information is being withheld from the consumer simply to benefit a food-processing industry that is responsible for more deaths around the world each year than probably everything else combined.

Trans-fatty acids have this deleterious effect on heart disease by increasing LDL (bad) cholesterol to the same extent that saturated fats do and by decreasing HDL (good) cholesterol—a heart-attack-waiting-to-happen double whammy. Also, trans-fatty acids raise lipoprotein(a) levels, impair arterial flexibility (helping to raise blood pressure and increase the risk for stroke), promote insulin resistance, and increase the risk for diabetes. Gee, that sounds an awful lot like the metabolic Syndrome X that's so prevalent in our society today. I wonder if it has anything to do with the processed foods that we consume? Studies show that people who consume large amounts of trans-fatty acids in their diet will more than double their heart-disease risk. You should avoid trans-fatty acids at all costs, but that's harder than you might think, considering that they're found in more than 42,000 foods in the United States alone. Trans-fatty acids are in 40 percent of all prepared foods, including cookies, crackers, chips, pastries, breakfast cereals, granola bars, and microwave popcorn, to name a few, according to the United States Department of Agriculture. They are also found in some frozen foods, such as pies and waffles.

Margarine, my second-worst food after canola oil, accounts for 20 to 30 percent of all trans-fatty acids consumed in the Untied States. The rest comes from shortening, baked goods, fast foods, and other junk food—essentially, any boxed food in your cupboard. So, go immediately to your cupboard and look at every canned, bagged, or boxed food, then throw away anything that has the words *partially hydrogenated or vegetable shortening* listed in the ingredients. The easiest way to avoid trans-fatty acids is to eat only whole, real foods—the Hamptons way.

Some food manufacturers, such as Kraft and Frito-Lay, have stated that they will voluntarily start to decrease the amount of trans-fats in their products. They're worried about huge lawsuits like those that roiled the cigarette industry. My only question is, Why did it take them so long? They had to know these fats were killing us. The FDA estimates that the change in regulations will save between $900 million and $1.8 billion a year in medical costs, lost productivity, and pain and suffering. When as little as 2 to 3 grams of trans-fats per day can increase health risks (for example, a doughnut has 4 grams), we're facing a serious dilemma in changing how we eat. Given the standard American diet, it's likely that trans-fat intake hovers at around 40 grams per day, with fast-food and junk-food eaters ingesting much more. Although the amount of trans-fats in animal products is not as high as in other foods, animal products do contain some trans-fats. Limit your consumption of animal product trans-fats by choosing lean cuts of beef, trimming the fat from pork, removing the skin from chicken, and selecting white meat instead of dark meat when eating poultry.

According to Dr. Walter Willett of Harvard, "Trans-fat is many times worse than saturated fat on a gram-for-gram basis." Dr. Willett published a study on trans-fats showing that women with the highest intake of trans-fats were 50 percent more likely to be diagnosed with heart disease than were women with the lowest intake. This study appeared in 1993 but with very little fanfare and public outcry. Subsequent studies also showed that trans-fats caused heart disease, yet most people still don't know how much of these fats they're eating because the information is not yet required to be listed on food labels.

For years, scientists lumped all fats together when considering disease rates, and they emphasized the health risks of saturated fats. Trans-fats were actually touted as heart-healthy, as was margarine, because neither was a saturated fat. Many low-fat foods, generating billions of dollars in sales, were riddled with trans-fatty acids. This occurred at the same time that natural foods, like eggs, which have been with us since the dawn of creation, were being derided as unhealthy. Given the data, it seems clear that the message should be to eat natural fats; oils that are highest in monounsaturated fat, such as macadamia nut oil; and butter instead of margarine. Yet there continues to be a dramatic rise in the consumption of polyunsaturated vegetable oils.

Dr. Willett states, "I think people shouldn't try to think of this as a trade-off between saturated fat and trans-fat—what you really want to go for is unsaturated fat." Australian macadamia nut oil is the gold standard of unsaturated fat. It is monounsaturated-rich and is not processed, except in the minimal way that any food must be processed to give us oil. This is the key to the Hamptons Diet: an encouragement to use monounsaturated fats, coupled with an emphasis on naturally occurring foods.

Skilled label sleuths won't have to wait until 2006 to figure out how many trans-fatty acids are in the foods they eat. If the Nutrition Facts box lists saturated fat, polyunsaturated fat, and monounsaturated fat, it's quite easy to figure out. Simply add the grams from those three categories, and subtract that total from the total grams of fat. The difference is the amount of trans-fats. Another thing to consider: heating an oil to a temperature above its smoke point leads to trans-fatty acid formation. Olive oil burns at 300 degrees F and shouldn't be used for sautéing. Australian macadamia nut oil burns at a higher temperature, 410 degrees F, so there is less concern about trans-fatty acid formation when cooking with this oil.

TRANS-FATS IN ONE SERVING OF SELECTED FOODS

Food	Trans-fat grams per serving
vegetable shortening	1.4–4.2
margarine (stick)	1.8–3.5
margarine (tub)	0.4–1.6
butter	0.3
vegetable oils	0.06
Macadamia nut oil	0
pound cake	4.3
doughnuts	3.8
french fries (fast food)	3.6
microwave popcorn	2.2

Source: United States Department of Agriculture

Eat Healthful Fats: Use Macadamia Nut Oil (Preferably) or Estate-Bottled Olive Oil

In the classic Mediterranean diet, olive oil is the oil of choice. In the Hamptons Diet, macadamia nut oil is the oil of choice.

These oils are both mostly monounsaturated (70 percent for olive and 85 percent for macadamia), with a predominance of oleic acid. Oleic acid increases the incorporation of omega-3 fatty acids into the cell membrane, perhaps decreasing the incidence of breast cancer. This fatty-acid profile has been shown to decrease total and LDL (bad) cholesterol levels to the same degree that low-fat diets do. However, these oils can also lower triglyceride levels and raise HDL (good) cholesterol levels, which low-fat diets (AHA Step II) cannot. Since macadamia nut oil is more monounsaturate-rich than olive oil is, it stands to reason that these cardiac and anticancer benefits would be even more pronounced in a diet that's higher in monounsaturated fats than the Mediterranean diet is—the Hamptons Diet.

The only healthy olive oils are estate-bottled, extra-virgin, single varietal oils. Similar to wine, each olive will have a distinctive flavor and be prized for different dishes. These oils are quite expensive but should be the ones you use if you choose olive oil. They have the highest smoke points, the lowest free fatty acid levels, the lowest acidity levels, and are higher in monounsaturated fat than other oils. The ordinary olive oils that most of us buy are poor quality blended oils that have very few health benefits. Because many of you will keep some olive oil on hand for using in your favorite Italian dishes or on salads, something I recently discovered bears mentioning—use Australian olive oil. Australian olives grow in a clean environment, good soil, and 46 percent extra sunshine. The oil made from these olives has to pass Australia's high processing standards, and the Australian truth-in-labeling laws decrease fraud and confusion in the Australian olive oil industry. Australian olive oil is my choice for olive oil if you are not using macadamia nut oil.

For simplicity's sake, know when choosing an olive oil that it is impossible to get an inexpensive, good quality extra-virgin olive oil. A low price should make you question the quality and even the purity of the oil. Most good, healthy olive oils will cost about $20 for 16 ounces, and many will cost much more than that.

It's still possible to use olive oil on the Hamptons Diet, if you must, but it should be an estate-bottled variety. After estate-bottled olive oil, the next best is almond or avocado oil. However, I must recommend that you use Australian macadamia nut oil as a first choice.

Consume Ample Quantities of Vegetables and Some Fruits

In several hundred studies, this has been shown to dramatically decrease your risk of developing cancer. Although *The Hamptons Diet* is primarily a weight-loss book, I want you to understand the scientific background behind my recommendations. Antioxidant vitamins and phytochemicals, which are found naturally in vegetables (as long as you don't overcook them) and fruits, are the key reasons why these foods are so healthy. Nutritional supplements can't possibly contain the same micronutrients found in fresh fruits and vegetables and thus will not have the same beneficial effect as the amount of fruits and vegetables recommended in the Hamptons Diet.

Consume Moderate Amounts of Alcohol

The cardio-protective effect of drinking moderate amounts of alcohol has been shown in multiple large epidemiological studies. The emphasis is on moderation. The results show that moderate drinkers (men who drank five to six drinks per week) had a 20 percent lower mortality rate from all causes and that they lived longer than those who drank less. Newer studies show that alcohol can improve insulin resistance and can prevent the onset of diabetes. The study also showed that diabetics who drink decrease their risk for heart disease even more than people who are not diabetic do. Obviously, though, an increase in the amount of alcohol consumed will incur less, not more, health benefits, because hypertension, liver disease, and cancer rates start to rise when you drink too much.

Carbohydrates Can Be Dangerous Too

Finally, we are beginning to understand the issue of carbohydrates. The USDA food pyramid has been an unmitigated disaster, and common sense is starting to prevail. In fact, a recent study proved that the increased consumption of refined carbohydrates is the primary cause of the obesity epidemic. I will soon unveil the Hamptons Diet Pyramids, which will explain the nutritional picture a lot better. The current "dietary wisdom," with an emphasis on eating carbohydrates of any kind and eliminating fat, no matter which kind, has been proven wrong. People simply substituted refined carbohydrates for fat. This dietary change was shown to raise triglyceride levels and lower total, as well as LDL (bad), cholesterol, resulting in no reduction of heart disease risk. Unrefined or whole grains are considered heart-healthy—in moderation, of course. Whole grains that are rich in soluble fiber, like oats and barley, are also cardio-protective.

Other important scientific findings that support the use of a Hamptons-type diet:

1. Triglyceride levels increase when dietary fats are replaced by carbohydrates. Therefore, eat good fats and decrease consumption of unhealthful simple carbohydrates.
2. Dietary cholesterol and moderate egg consumption were not significantly associated with heart disease or stroke. Moderate was defined as seven eggs per week. Eggs are a good source of lean protein.

CHAPTER 4

The Hamptons Diet Pyramids

Marge became a patient around the time of menopause. Over the years, she had gradually gained some weight, especially around the midsection. She admitted to being thirty-five pounds heavier than when she got married—a relatively common occurrence after the birth of two children. Yet Marge was not an obese gal. She still played tennis and enjoyed the cocktail party circuit. She was the wife of a very successful entrepreneur who made millions in Hamptons real estate deals, and she needed to look her best. I explained the concepts of the Hamptons Diet, telling her that this lower-carbohydrate approach allows good, healthful complex carbohydrates, but in limited quantities, and permits unlimited amounts of very satisfying foods. She sat there and listened and then asked, "How is this different from any other low-carbohydrate diet?"

I said I could promise her something that no other low-carbohydrate diet could. I would make her richer if she ate this way. "Go on," she said. "Monounsaturated-rich," I countered. She liked the idea of having more fat in her diet. She had tried fat-restricted diets before and was never satisfied because she was limited to eating very few calories in order to lose a tiny amount of weight each week. She had also tried very low-carbohydrate diets and found that they had too much fat, leaving her with an uncomfortable feeling after a meal. She couldn't get it out of her head that so much meat was bad for her.

She was intrigued by my description of the Hamptons Diet and revealed that her parents had never worried about fat. They ate red meat sometimes three times a day and lived to their nineties. Why did she worry about everything and gain weight at the same time? After hearing of the wonders of the Hamptons Diet, she couldn't wait to get started. In just five months, she lost all thirty-five extra pounds, and she looked and felt terrific. She couldn't believe that it was so easy because she always ate well and never felt hungry.

Making the Pyramids User-Friendly

Yes, I intentionally pluralized the word *Pyramid.* Nutrition is an extremely complex and evolving science; in my opinion, one pyramid cannot possibly convey a positive health message. Science knows more now than ever before about the micronutrients of foods and how these play a role in health. Therefore, it's impossible to create one pyramid to teach you how to eat. I have been an outspoken critic of the USDA food pyramid for years, so there's no further need to discuss my views here. In my pyramid system, I've broken down foods by categories and devised a pyramid for each type. So, you can quickly figure out whether a carbohydrate or a protein is healthful simply by glancing at or memorizing these pyramids; they're not that complicated.

The Protein Pyramid

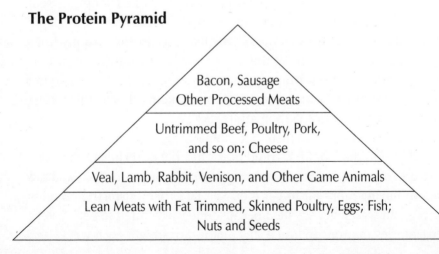

Bacon, Sausage
Other Processed Meats

Untrimmed Beef, Poultry, Pork,
and so on; Cheese

Veal, Lamb, Rabbit, Venison, and Other Game Animals

Lean Meats with Fat Trimmed, Skinned Poultry, Eggs; Fish;
Nuts and Seeds

In this pyramid, all foods are permitted, but it's best to limit the top two tiers and try to eat more of the foods on the bottom rungs.

The Carbohydrate (Grains) Pyramid

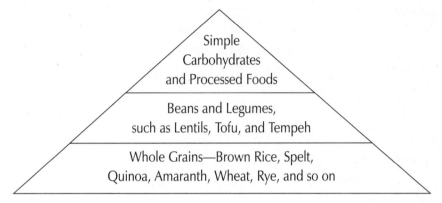

In this pyramid, you should completely avoid the top tier. Beans, legumes, and whole grains are included in the Hamptons Diet in varying amounts, depending on how much weight you have to lose. All of the details will be explained in a later chapter.

The Carbohydrate (Vegetables) Pyramid

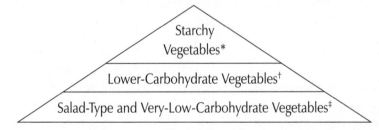

For this pyramid, simply avoid the top tier while you're trying to lose weight, and then later incorporate these into your diet program. When

---

*Starchy vegetables are peas, carrots, corn, potatoes (white), winter squash (butternut, buttercup, etc.), beets, parsnips, jicama, breadfruit, cassava, plantains, and christophene.
†Lower-carbohydrate vegetables include eggplant, onion, tomato, broccoli, cauliflower, asparagus, cabbage, leeks, scallions, water chestnuts, zucchini, string beans, avocados, spaghetti squash, turnips, artichoke hearts, okra, collard greens, and dandelion greens.
‡Salad vegetables include lettuces of all types, spinach, kale, fennel, mushrooms, bok choy, celery, radishes, peppers, bean sprouts, and cucumbers.

you want to maintain your weight loss, keep in mind that not all vegetables are created equal, so this pyramid helps you sort through the
various types. The same holds true for the following fruit pyramid. All
fruits can be eaten, but try to eat more from the lower rungs of the
ladder.

These lists are not meant to be exhaustive; there are more lists
in a subsequent chapter. Just remember this simple rule: If the
vegetable isn't listed on the top or the bottom rung, then it's on the
middle rung.

The Fruit Pyramid

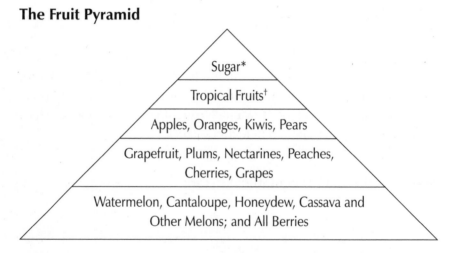

You are encouraged to eat all of the fruits on the Hamptons Diet; just
focus on some more than on others in the initial weight-loss phase of
the dieting process. This pyramid illustrates how to think of food after
you have lost weight. The weight loss rules will soon follow.

---

*Sugar includes but is not limited to corn syrup, beet sugar, maple syrup, fructose,
high-fructose corn syrup, sucrose, cane sugar, brown rice syrup, brown sugar, honey,
and any other disguised form of sugar.
†Tropical fruits include bananas, pineapples, guavas, mangos, papayas, passion fruit,
and so on.

The Fats and Oil Pyramid

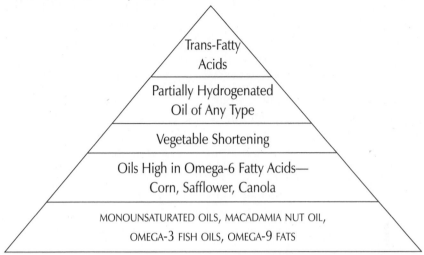

This pyramid is simple but crucial, if you want to maintain optimal health, and is the primary reason why the Hamptons Diet has been such a success for my patients. So study it and take careful note of the healthful fats and oils. Use only oils from the bottom rung of this pyramid.

Steve, a well-known Hollywood-type who has a home in the Hamptons, wanted to get healthier. Since most of his friends were my clients, he decided to come in and see what all the fuss was about. Two of his leading ladies had lost weight on the Hamptons Diet, and several others in his tight-knit party circuit of friends had as well. What could I possibly be telling them that he didn't already know? He didn't need to lose weight, but he had high cholesterol and didn't want to have a heart attack. Steve followed a pretty strict low-fat diet regimen. He employed a cook, so it was easy for him to follow any program. He exercised regularly because this lucky fellow had a small town–sized mansion right on the beach, and he liked to jog early every morning.

No matter how much fat he cut out of his diet, it seemed that his cholesterol kept going up. It was a slow process, but over the years it had risen 55 points and was now at the stage where his physician wanted him to begin taking medication. Many of his polo buddies had come off high cholesterol medications simply by following my advice.

HAMPTONS DIET ACCEPTABLE AND UNACCEPTABLE FOODS LIST

Food Type	Eat	Don't Eat
protein	lean meat with the fat trimmed, poultry without the skin	untrimmed meats, too much bacon/sausage or milk
fish or omega-3 fatty acids	salmon, trout, sardines, flaxseeds, walnuts	fried fish (unless unbreaded and pan seared in macadamia nut oil)
fruits and vegetables	lots of vegetables, and limit fruits to those that are low in sugar	high-sugar fruits like bananas; limit corn, peas, tomatoes, and potatoes.
beans, legumes, and nuts	macadamia, brazil, walnut, pecan, lentils, beans	honey-roasted nuts; limit peanuts and peas.
grains	whole grains only— the word *whole* must appear on the ingredient list, not just on the label	white flour products, including rice and pasta, biscuits, refined carbohydrates, and processed foods
oils	macadamia nut oil— use extra virgin, estate-bottled olive oil or avocado oil as a second choice	every other oil, bar none, including any types of spreads or margarine
fats	monounsaturated-rich; emphasize whole foods and no trans-fatty acids	no fried fast food, chips, crackers, or packaged or processed foods of any kind; read labels to avoid anything that is hydrogenated.
alcohol	5 oz of wine, 1.5 oz of distilled spirits	limit to two of these for women and four of these servings for men per week.

He wanted this result, too, and since my name kept coming up every-where he turned, he sought my advice.

I basically explained to him everything about fats that you have just read. He wasn't completely convinced, despite all the scientific lit-erature. Steve was incredibly rich, yet he needed to realize that he had to be monounsaturated-rich as well. He agreed to follow my dietary advice for six weeks and then have a blood test to see whether the diet had worked. I told him that six weeks wasn't enough time, but he's the sort of guy you just don't say no to. I had to perform as well as any of his other performers did. It wasn't a role I normally like, but it *was* a challenge I knew I could meet.

By the end of six weeks, Steve remarked on how easy the Hamp-tons Diet was. He had never been hungry the way he always was on his low-fat regimen, and he could exercise more than before because of his increased energy. He thought the diet would be hard to follow, but I gave him this table, which helped him to categorize foods quite easily.

Steve lost about 5 pounds, his cholesterol dropped 40 points, and his HDL went up by 25 points to a respectable number of 50. He was quite pleased and now knew what all the fuss was about regarding the Hamptons Diet.

So what is the Hamptons Diet? I'm not advocating a high-fat, ultra–low carbohydrate approach as the most healthful. I recommend an approach that is low in processed foods; high in good sources of protein; rich in vegetables, nuts, and low-sugar fruits; and rich in omega-9 monounsaturated fats.

The Hamptons Diet doesn't require a radical shift in eating behavior, just a shift toward more healthful choices. Extreme dietary modifications are basically impractical for most of us to maintain on a long-term basis. That's not to say that I encourage you to immedi-ately go back to your old ways once you've lost the weight you wish to lose. Since most of us have horrendous eating habits, for some peo-ple this may be a major shift; for others, it will just encourage them to make the correct decisions about food for a good part of the rest of their lives. No one is perfect, but if we aim for perfection and only get to 80 percent, we have still made a big difference in our health-risk factors.

The Hamptons Heart-Healthy Diet
Top Ten Rules

1. Use Australian macadamia nut oil as your main source of monounsaturated fat.
2. Avoid sugar.
3. Avoid trans-fatty acids, which are found primarily in processed foods. Look for foods containing "partially hydrogenated" anything, margarine, or shortenings, and avoid them.
4. Avoid simple carbohydrates—this means nothing white, including pretzels, bagels, most breads, pasta, and rice.
5. Avoid oils that are high in omega-6 fatty acids, such as corn, sunflower, safflower, soybean, peanut, grapeseed, and highly processed oils like canola and most olive oils.
6. Incorporate more fatty fish into your diet, and if you can't, take a nutritional supplement that has the correct amounts of omega-3 fatty acids. Supplements will be explained in a subsequent chapter.
7. Eat nuts, legumes, and beans in moderation and as snacks.
8. Eat only whole grains, when eating grains.
9. Eat vegetables to excess, and limit fruits to those that contain the least amount of sugar.
10. Drink moderate amounts of alcohol.

CHAPTER 5

Choosing the Right
Oils and Fats

Deanna, a well-known actress who recently bought a house in East Hampton, came to see me for some good nutritional advice. Like most women, she wanted to drop a few pounds and was tired of having to starve herself to do it. She had a plum role that started filming at the end of the summer and she had eight weeks to look her best. She had been on the party circuit ever since arriving from the West Coast and was in serious danger from overexposure. She had been spotted at all the local charity events, art openings, and all the late-night beach parties. The local tabloid, *Dan's Papers,* followed her everywhere and even they were commenting on the weight she had put on ever since coming East. She admitted to me that she couldn't zip many of her dresses, and remember, this was coming from a woman who was already a toothpick.

She wanted me to tell her people exactly what to do to get her looking her optimal best. When I examined her, I noticed that she had some minor skin problems. When I mentioned this to her she said she had had those problems ever since puberty but since they were always covered up by makeup, she didn't mind them.

I told Deanna that most skin irritations were a direct result of something internal and that once she started the Hamptons Diet, her skin too would improve. She was more interested in losing weight so she really didn't give this any further thought. Deanna admitted that like many other people in Hollywood, she had tried a variety of different high-protein diets, but she didn't do well on them; she always felt full and tended to gain weight on them. I explained to her that although my approach was lower in carbs, it was all about the right carbohydrates and more about becoming monounsaturated-rich. So, I outlined the program, gave her her first bottle of Australian macadamia nut oil to take to her cook, and away she went.

After three weeks, she came into the city to see me and couldn't believe she had lost the eight pounds that she thought was going to take the rest of the summer to lose. She had never lost weight so fast in her life. Plus, in those three weeks, her face cleared up completely—it had never done that. I explained that was because macadamia nut oil was high in palmitoleic acid, a close relative to our own skin oil. Needless to say, she was pleased. The real key to weight-loss success is to design a diet that embraces healthy types of fat and healthy carbohydrates—the Hamptons way.

Since so many edible oils are on the market today, and seemingly new ones come along every few months, I've included a section in this book that describes the various oils. Now you can make an educated choice if you don't like the taste of macadamia nut oil or prefer to use something else from time to time. If you only want to know which one to use and when to use it, just take the advice of Jenny, who was thrilled to lose 110 pounds on the Hamptons Diet in nine months: "Use macadamia oil for everything—it changed my life." She went from a size 24 to a size 12—she lost an entire person. When I explain to my patients which fats and oils to use, the message is clear: Macadamia nut oil for every culinary use; butter instead of margarine when you want a spread; no polyunsaturated oils; and no trans-fats. Once Jenny made these changes to her diet, her allergies completely disappeared and she started to lose weight—sixteen pounds in the first two weeks alone. So, I know that she is a convert, but what about you? I need to convince you, and since you might want to try different oils in recipes from time to time, it's important that you know what you're getting when you purchase a product.

Here is a simple cheat sheet to keep in mind when buying a fat or an oil:

- Monounsaturated fats = healthful = omega-9 fatty acids
- Polyunsaturated fats must be balanced or they are unhealthful. These include omega-3 and omega-6 fatty acids—look for that 1:1 ratio of the omega-6 to omega-3 fatty acids, or as close to 1:1 as possible
- Trans-fats = deadly
- Smoke points = the higher, the better
- Oxidation = the slower, the better

Understanding Oils

In an attempt to make this easier to understand, I've broken down the following oils into five categories.

Category 1: Low Smoke-Point Oils

These oils should never be heated. They are meant to be used as nutritional supplements for their fatty-acid content. The two most common examples are flaxseed oil and omega-3 fish oils. Keep in mind that the smoke points given in this chapter are averages, based on all the information that I have gathered. Each oil seems to have a range, most likely based on the oil's age and the lab doing the testing. Some low-temperature cooking uses include salad dressings, steaming, simmering, and parboiling. However, I would never use this group for anything except cold recipes.

Flaxseed Oil

The richest source of the omega-3 fatty acid ALA, flaxseed oil is also the highest plant-based source of omega-3 fatty acids. This oil should never be used for cooking. It must be refrigerated and will last for only two months once opened. It can be stored in the freezer to prolong its shelf life, but I recommend keeping it open for just two months and then using it on your wood cabinets after that—it makes a perfect polish. Another way to obtain the benefits of flaxseed oil is to grind the seeds yourself each morning in a coffee grinder, being careful not to overgrind, as this can increase the heat and break down the fatty acid content.

- omega-6 to omega-3 ratio = 0.3:1 (excellent)

- omega-3 content = 57%
- omega-6 content = 16%
- omega-9 content = 18%
- saturated fat = 9%
- smoke point = 225 degrees F

Fish Oil

This oil is usually composed of the oils of assorted cold-water fish, such as salmon, mackerel, herring, and sardines. It can never be used for cooking and should be stored in the refrigerator. It is generally consumed in the form of a nutritional supplement. Since we are so omega-3 deprived, most of us will need to take one of these supplements at the start of the Hamptons Diet to ensure that we combat the high levels of omega-6 fatty acids coursing through our bodies. The fatty-acid content will vary, according to which types of fish have been used.

- omega-6 to omega-3 ratio = not a source of omega-6 fatty acids
- omega-3 content = 75%
- omega-6 content = 0%
- omega-9 content = 0%
- saturated fat = 25%
- smoke point = 235 degrees F

Borage Oil

This oil is a source of the omega-6 fatty acid called GLA and contains twice as much as evening primrose oil does. Borage oil should never be used for cooking. It's taken in the form of a nutritional supplement. GLA is one of the healthful omega-6 fatty acids.

- omega-6 to omega-3 ratio = not a source of omega-3 fatty acids
- omega-3 fatty acids = 0%
- omega-6 fatty acids = 60%, but only 22% healthful omega-6
- omega-9 fatty acids = 26%
- saturated fat = 14%
- smoke point = 225 degrees F

Evening Primrose Oil

This is another rich source of the omega-6 fatty acid GLA. It should not be used in cooking.

- omega-6 to omega-3 ratio = not a source of omega-3 fatty acids
- omega-3 fatty acids = 0%
- omega-6 fatty acids = 81%, but only 9% healthful omega-6
- omega-9 fatty acids = 9%
- saturated fat = 10%
- smoke point = 225 degrees F

Wheat Germ Oil

This oil contains some omega-3 fatty acids but is overwhelmingly an omega-6 fatty acid. It should never be used for cooking. Most people get it in supplement form by the name of octacosanol. Therefore, if you're taking this supplement, you need to increase your intake of omega-3 fats to balance it out.

- omega-6 to omega-3 ratio = 6.5:1
- omega-3 fatty acids = 8%
- omega-6 fatty acids = 53%
- omega-9 fatty acids = 22%
- saturated fat = 17%
- smoke point = 225 degrees F

Hemp Seed Oil

This oil is not widely used and should never be heated. It is a rich source of the omega-3 fatty acid ALA.

- omega-6 to omega-3 ratio = 2.5:1
- omega-3 fatty acids = 21%
- omega-6 fatty acids = 54%
- omega-9 fatty acids = 15%
- saturated fat = 10%
- smoke point = 225–300 degrees F

Black Currant Oil

This is another decent source of GLA but without any trace of omega-3 fatty acid. It should never be used for cooking.

- omega-6 to omega-3 ratio = not an appreciable source of omega-3 fatty acids
- omega-3 fatty acids = 0%

- omega-6 fatty acids = 80%, of which only 18% is GLA
- omega-9 fatty acids = 12%
- saturated fat = 8%
- smoke point = 225 degrees F

Other low smoke-point oils (not that I condone their use, mind you) include

- unrefined canola oil
- unrefined safflower oil
- unrefined sunflower oil

Category 2: Medium Smoke-Point Oils

You can cook with these oils only at your own risk. Their smoke points lend them to light sautéing, low-heat baking, and pressure cooking—methods where the temperature stays below 320 degrees F. Most of these oils are unrefined and will have some flavor because of that. Some oils in this category are semirefined. The more refined the oil, the more it has been subjected to processing and the less healthful it is. Some of these oils will be mentioned in different categories, because this section is set up only according to smoke point. The fatty-acid profile of each oil is different, so pay attention to that. Olive oil is in this category.

Corn Oil

This is an old favorite and was the second-most commonly used oil in my household when I was growing up—with olive oil being the first, of course. It contains a scant amount of omega-3 fatty acids and is almost entirely omega-6 polyunsaturated fat. The smoke point is for the unrefined version. It should never be used for deep frying because of its tendency to foam. If you want to bake with it in the oven, never use temperatures greater than 350 degrees F.

- omega-6 to omega-3 ratio = 59:1 (pathetic)
- omega-3 fatty acids = 1%
- omega-6 fatty acids = 59%
- omega-9 fatty acids = 27%
- saturated fat = 13%
- smoke point = 320 degrees F

Peanut Oil

This is high in monounsaturated fat but not as high as macadamia nut oil—or olive oil, for that matter. I recommend this oil only if it's organic and only on rare occasions, since it has high levels of omega-6 fats, despite the monounsaturated fat content. The smoke point is only for the unrefined version of the oil.

- omega-6 to omega-3 ratio = 34:1
- omega-3 fatty acids = 0%
- omega-6 fatty acids = 34%
- omega-9 fatty acids = 48%
- saturated fat = 18%
- smoke point = 275–300 degrees F

Sesame Oil

This oil is used extensively in Asian and Middle Eastern cuisine, so you will get it when you eat in these types of restaurants. Sesame oil contains some monounsaturated fats but is high in omega-6 polyunsaturated fats. Some of sesame oil's health benefits are due to its unique antioxidants, which are not destroyed by heat. This may be due to the sesamol. Sesame oil also contains phosphatidyl choline, so this oil is not all bad. Limit its use to *rarely,* since it does have a high amount of omega-6 polyunsaturates.

- omega-6 to omega-3 ratio = 45:1
- omega-3 fatty acids = 0%
- omega-6 fatty acids = 45%
- omega-9 fatty acids = 40%
- saturated fat = 15%
- smoke point = 250–300 degrees F

Soybean Oil

This oil doesn't tolerate heat well and is better used cold, if at all. Soybean oil is almost always refined and is hydrogenated or partially hydrogenated into shortenings, margarines, or (usually) salad dressings. For those reasons, and because most of the soybean crop in this country is genetically modified, I recommend avoiding this oil.

- omega-6 to omega-3 ratio = 11:1

- omega-3 fatty acids = 5%
- omega-6 fatty acids = 56%
- omega-9 fatty acids = 24%
- saturated fat = 15%
- smoke point = 300 degrees F

Safflower Oil

This oil comes in many different varieties now. It was very popular in the 1970s, when the benefits of polyunsaturated fats were being touted, as this oil contains the highest percentage of polyunsaturated fats. I think this oil is quite undesirable because it oxidizes extremely rapidly.

- omega-6 to omega-3 ratio = 78:1 (the worst)
- omega-3 fatty acids = 0%
- omega-6 fatty acids = 78%
- omega-9 fatty acids = 14%
- saturated fat = 8%
- smoke point = 300 degrees F

High-Oleic Safflower Oil

This oil comes from a new strain of seed that was developed to have more monounsaturated fats—another example of "frankenfoods." Its high levels of monounsaturated fats (oleic acid) allow it to undergo much less oxidation, but I don't recommend this oil because of its genetic manipulation and because the smoke point still remains low.

- omega-6 to omega-3 ratio = 16:1
- omega-3 fatty acids = 0%
- omega-6 fatty acids = 16%
- omega-9 fatty acids = 76%
- saturated fat = 8%
- smoke point = 325 degrees F

Sunflower Oil

This is second to safflower oil in the amount of polyunsaturated fats. It is extremely unstable and is found only in refined versions because of its tendency toward oxidation. It is not a heathful oil to use.

- omega-6 to omega-3 ratio = 69:1

- omega-3 fatty acids = 0%
- omega-6 fatty acids = 69%
- omega-9 fatty acids = 19%
- saturated fat = 12%
- smoke point = 300 degrees F

High-Oleic Sunflower Oil

As with safflower oil, a new breed of seed was developed whose fatty-acid content was made much less sensitive to oxidation and much higher in monounsaturated fats. Again, I don't recommend the use of this oil at all, as it has been refined and has a low smoke point.

- omega-6 to omega-3 ratio = 6.5:1
- omega-3 fatty acids = 0%
- omega-6 fatty acids = 11%
- omega-9 fatty acids = 81%
- saturated fat = 8%
- smoke point = 325 degrees F

Walnut Oil

Since most walnuts used for oil are highly processed, the desirability of walnut oil diminishes. If you can find an organic version, you may want to occasionally use this in salad dressings or a light sauté. The oil contains a minor amount of omega-3 fatty acids but is essentially a polyunsaturated fat. So, if you do decide to use this oil, use it sparingly.

- omega-6 to omega-3 ratio = 6.8:1
- omega-3 fatty acids = 5%
- omega-6 fatty acids = 58%, 3% of which is GLA
- omega-9 fatty acids = 28%
- saturated fat = 9%
- smoke point = 320 degrees F

Pumpkinseed Oil

This oil does contain some omega-3 fatty acids and some monounsaturated fats, but it still has a poor ratio.

- omega-6 to omega-3 ratio = 20:1
- omega-3 fatty acids = 3%

- omega-6 fatty acids = 60%
- omega-9 fatty acids = 20%
- saturated fat = 17%
- smoke point = 250 degrees F

Pistachio Oil

This oil has a high percentage of monounsaturated fat but also has many polyunsaturated fats.

- omega-6 to omega-3 ratio = 31:1
- omega-3 fatty acids = 0%
- omega-6 fatty acids = 31%
- omega-9 fatty acids = 54%
- saturated fat = 15%
- smoke point = 325–350 degrees F

Olive Oil

I am listing the fatty-acid profiles here for comparison; pay careful attention to the ratio.

- omega-6 to omega-3 ratio = 12:1
- omega-3 fatty acids = 1%
- omega-6 fatty acids = 12%
- omega-9 fatty acids = 72%
- saturated fat = 15%
- smoke point = 250–300 degrees F

Category 3: High Smoke-Point Oils

If so inclined, you can use the oils in this category for most baking purposes, as well as for sautéing, stir-frying, and wok cooking, strictly from a smoke-point perspective. However, these oils are either semi-refined or completely refined, so I don't recommend their use. Some of the fatty-acid profiles of the oils in this category have been described previously. The higher smoke points of these oils are simply due to the oil being more refined and less healthful.

Cottonseed Oil

This oil is not widely available for consumer use and is almost exclusively used as an ingredient in processed foods. It has a long history of use in this country, since the 1860s, when cotton was king, and was the source of the first Crisco ever made, in 1911. It is used in processed foods because of its high smoke point and its ability to increase shelf life due to its being hydrogenated. The saturated fat that it contains is palmitic acid, which has been shown to elevate cholesterol. Because of its level of hydrogenation, cottonseed oil contains many trans-fatty acids. Avoid this killer.

- omega-6 to omega-3 ratio = 56:1
- omega-3 fatty acids = 0%
- omega-6 fatty acids = 56%
- omega-9 fatty acids = 18%
- saturated fat = 26%
- smoke point = 400 degrees F

Grapeseed Oil

This oil is made from the seeds of grapes after the wine is pressed. Most grapeseed oil that's on the market has been chemically extracted. The ratios are not impressive, either. I would never use this oil in my own kitchen, and I don't recommend that you cook with it, either. Its supposed health benefits are vastly overrated.

- omega-6 to omega-3 ratio = 76:1
- omega-3 fatty acids = 0%
- omega-6 fatty acids = 76%
- omega-9 fatty acids = 15%
- saturated fat = 9%
- smoke point = 400 degrees F

Tea Seed or Camellia Oil

This is a new type of oil from China. I hesitate to recommend it because it's being touted as the answer to everything, as both medicine and health food, so I'm a little skeptical. However, to be complete, I include it here.

- omega-6 to omega-3 ratio = 8:1
- omega-3 fatty acids = 0%
- omega-6 fatty acids = 9%
- omega-9 fatty acids = 83%

- saturated fat = 8%
- smoke point = 400 degrees F

Canola Oil

This oil is included so that you can compare the profiles more easily. I would never use this oil.

- omega-6 to omega-3 ratio = 2.4:1
- omega-3 fatty acids = 10%
- omega-6 fatty acids = 24%
- omega-9 fatty acids = 54%
- saturated fat = 12%
- smoke point = 350 degrees F

Here are the other oils in this category whose fatty acid profiles were described previously. These have all been further refined to achieve higher smoke points.

Refined corn oil = 375–400 degrees F

Refined safflower oil = 350 degrees F

Refined sesame oil = 350 degrees F

Semirefined high-oleic sunflower oil = 375 degrees F

Semirefined soybean oil = 350 degrees F

Refined soybean oil = 400 degrees F

Semirefined walnut oil = 400 degrees F

Refined peanut oil = 400 degrees F

Semirefined sunflower oil = 400 degrees F

Refined canola oil = 400 degrees F

Category 4: Ultra-High Smoke-Point Oils

This is my favorite category of oil because I get to talk about the basis for the Hamptons Diet—macadamia nut oil. Macadamia nut oil fits in this category, but so do a few other oils. Most are refined, but some, like Australian macadamia nut oil, are not. These oils have very high smoke points and can be used for searing, browning, deep-frying, making tempura and breaded foods, and high-temperature baking.

Maria couldn't wait to start her diet. All of her friends had lost weight on my program, and she wanted to be next. She had one little problem—she was afraid to switch to macadamia nut oil. She had always used olive oil and thought it was the most healthful. Besides, she was of Latin heritage and couldn't see making the switch; nothing would taste right. To be perfectly honest, she was a bit of a diva—not only in real life but by profession. I explained that the key to the Hamptons Diet, the reason it works so well, is the perfect health profile of its star ingredient—Australian premium macadamia nut oil. She reluctantly agreed to use it, but mostly because all of her girl-friends had made the switch. Three months, six dress sizes, and thirty pounds later, she couldn't be happier.

Let's simply start with the oils I've already mentioned that have been further refined to get higher smoke points.

Refined high-oleic safflower = 450 degrees F

Refined high-oleic sunflower = 450 degrees F

Highly refined peanut = 450 degrees F

Highly refined soybean = 450 degrees F

Macadamia Nut Oil

This oil contains the highest amount of monounsaturated fats on the market, making it extremely stable; it has a high smoke point and has the perfect fatty-acid ratio of 1:1 that we're striving for.

- omega-6 to omega-3 ratio = 1:1
- omega-3 fatty acids = 2%
- omega-6 fatty acids = 2%
- omega-9 fatty acids = 84%
- saturated fat = 12%
- smoke point = 400–450 degrees F

Almond Oil

Like most oils made from nuts, this has a high smoke point and good levels of monounsaturated fats, but it still has a moderate level of polyunsaturates.

- omega-6 to omega-3 ratio = 28:1
- omega-3 fatty acids = 0%
- omega-6 fatty acids = 28%

- omega-9 fatty acids = 65%
- saturated fat = 7%
- smoke point = 430 degrees F

Hazelnut Oil

This nut oil contains a very high amount of monounsaturated fats, but its polyunsaturated fat content remains a little high, thus making it an unwise choice for your table.

- omega-6 to omega-3 ratio = 15:1
- omega-3 fatty acids = 0%
- omega-6 fatty acids = 15%
- omega-9 fatty acids = 75%
- saturated fat = 10%
- smoke point = 425 degrees F

Palm Oil or Palm Kernel Oil

Palm oil is isolated from the pulp of the oil palm tree, and palm kernel oil is derived from the kernel. They have slightly different fatty-acid profiles because of this, but they're both high in saturated fat. Don't fear these oils unless they have been hydrogenated. Because they don't contain significant amounts of monounsaturated fats, however, I don't recommend their use on a regular basis or their inclusion in the Hamptons Diet.

For palm oil:

- omega-6 to omega-3 ratio = 10:1
- omega-3 fatty acids = 0%
- omega-6 fatty acids = 10%
- omega-9 fatty acids = 39%
- saturated fat = 51%
- smoke point = 450 degrees F

For palm kernel oil:

- omega-6 to omega-3 ratio = 2:1
- omega-3 fatty acids = 0%
- omega-6 fatty acids = 2%
- omega-9 fatty acids = 14%

- saturated fat = 84%
- smoke point = 450 degrees F

Coconut Oil

This is another misunderstood fat. It is derived from the coconut meat. It's not unhealthful unless it has been hydrogenated. Although it's not as good as macadamia nut oil, for many reasons, it isn't as bad as it's made out to be. This oil is rich in saturated fats and contains no appreciable amount of unsaturated fatty acids. It is extremely stable at high temperatures and has a low degree of oxidation. However, most research shows that coconut oil increases cholesterol levels and ratios.

- omega-6 to omega-3 ratio = there are no appreciable omega-3s
- omega-3 fatty acids = 0%
- omega-6 fatty acids = 1%
- omega-9 fatty acids = 8%
- saturated fat = 91%
- smoke point = 450 degrees F

Apricot Kernel Oil

As its name implies, this oil is made from the pits of apricots. Because of that, it has a high smoke point, but the fatty-acid ratio is not conducive to good health.

- omega-6 to omega-3 ratio = 31:1
- omega-3 fatty acids = 0%
- omega-6 fatty acids = 31%
- omega-9 fatty acids = 63%
- saturated fat = 6%
- smoke point = 495 degrees F

Rice Bran Oil

This oil is made from the outer bran of rice. It has a high smoke point but not much else going for it.

- omega-6 to omega-3 ratio = 27:1
- omega-3 fatty acids = 1%
- omega-6 fatty acids = 27%

- omega-9 fatty acids = 46%
- saturated fat = 26%
- smoke point = 490 degrees F

Avocado Oil

Although the monounsaturated fat content of avocado oil is high, it's still not as high as that of olive or macadamia nut oil. It also has the highest smoke point of any plant oil, and it is my solid second choice for use in the Hamptons Diet.

- omega-6 to omega-3 ratio = 18:1
- omega-3 fatty acids = 0%
- omega-6 fatty acids = 18%
- omega-9 fatty acids = 65%
- saturated fat = 17%
- smoke point = 520 degrees F

Super Canola Oil

This is a relatively new man-made invention. It is highly refined canola oil made from a variety of rape seed that has been formulated to produce a different fatty-acid profile. So, although it appears to fit my criteria for a healthful product, you must consider the processing that brought the oil to this state. Nothing this highly processed is ever healthful for you. In my opinion, it's as poisonous as the other canola oils are.

- omega-6 to omega-3 ratio = 1.6:1
- omega-3 fatty acids = 6%
- omega-6 fatty acids = 10%
- omega-9 fatty acids = 75%
- saturated fat = 9%
- smoke point = 520 degrees F

Category 5: Solid Fats

Many fats fit into this category, and most of them are traditional foods that have been used in cooking for centuries. However, some are man-made, manipulated food products. I will mention these only briefly, as they are not a large segment of what we cook with. Many of you may never use these products. They include butter, lard or pork fat, chicken fat, beef tallow and suet, duck and goose fat, and—the least healthful of them all—vegetable shortenings and margarine.

Smoke-Point Table

The following table shows the smoke points of oils and some fats. Please remember that the smoke point is not the only factor to consider when deciding which oil is right for your kitchen. The correct choice—and the key to weight loss and good health—is Australian macadamia nut oil. As a comparison, look at each oil's smoke point (macadamia's is highest), level of monounsaturated fats (macadamia's is high) and the ratio of omega-6 to omega-3 fatty acids (macadamia's is 1:1). Each oil has a range of smoke points, depending on the plant's growing conditions. The following chart simply lists an average.

Oil or Fat	Smoke Point (in degrees F)
flaxseed oil	225
black currant oil	225
wheat germ oil	225
evening primrose oil	225
borage oil	225
fish oil (blend)	235
hemp seed oil	250
sesame oil	250
peanut oil	275
soybean oil	300
safflower oil	300
sunflower oil	300
olive oil	300
pumpkin seed oil	250
walnut oil	320
corn oil	320
high-oleic safflower oil	325
high-oleic sunflower oil	325
pistachio oil	325

(continued)

Oil or Fat	Smoke Point (in degrees F)
canola oil	350
semirefined soybean oil	350
refined sesame oil	350
refined safflower oil	350
butter	350
lard	365
chicken fat	375
duck/goose fat	375
refined corn oil	375
semirefined high-oleic sunflower oil	375
beef tallow	400
refined soybean oil	400
semirefined walnut oil	400
refined peanut oil	400
semirefined sunflower oil	400
refined canola oil	400
cottonseed oil	400
grapeseed oil	400
tea seed/camellia oil	400
macadamia nut oil	400
hazelnut oil	425
almond oil	430
refined high-oleic safflower oil	450
refined high-oleic sunflower oil	450
highly refined peanut oil	450
highly refined soybean oil	450
palm oil	450
coconut oil	450
apricot kernel oil	495
rice bran oil	500
avocado oil	520
super canola oil	520

Understanding Fats

As you can see, this business of oils and fats doesn't get any easier when you begin to learn more about them. However, it's crucial to know about fats as we move into the next era of dieting—the Hamptons era.

Monounsaturated Fats

I've fully discussed how important these are in your diet. The essence of the Hamptons Diet is to become monounsaturated-rich. These fats don't turn rancid easily when used in cooking, and they are the main component of macadamia nut oil. Other oils that contain significantly less oleic acid are olive, almond, peanut, cashew, and avocado oils. Oleic acid is an important fatty acid, because it is an 18-carbon neutral, or an omega-9, acid. Therefore, your body isn't harmed when you consume this type of oil.

Polyunsaturated Fats

These fats have two or more double bonds. Because of these double bonds, all polyunsaturated oils are liquid at room temperature and remain liquid even in the refrigerator. The extra double bonds make these oils chemically unstable and more prone to attack by free radicals. They go rancid easily and should never be heated or used for cooking.

For years, polyunsaturated fatty acids were the darlings of the medical community, based on the antiquated notion that they had to be good for you because they are low in saturated fats. New research shows that the various polyunsaturated oils can have dramatically different effects on one's health, depending on their ratio of omega-6 to omega-3 fatty acids.

As you've seen, oils that contain a high percentage of polyunsaturated fatty acids include corn, safflower, sunflower, peanut, cottonseed, grapeseed, soybean (the most common oils on the market today), fish, walnut, and flaxseed oil. Brazil nuts, pistachios, pumpkin seeds, and sesame seeds are all high in polyunsaturated omega-6 fats. Flaxseed and fish oil are the most highly unsaturated oils of them all, and for our purposes, they are excluded from the discussions on unhealthful polyunsaturated fats. Fish oil is predominantly omega-3 fats, and flaxseed oil is the richest source of alpha-linolenic acid (ALA), another omega-3 fatty acid.

This chart lists the oils most commonly used and which category they fall into. Now you know which ones to get rid of immediately.

Omega-3 oils	Omega-6 oils
fish oils	corn oil
EPA	safflower oil
DHA	GLA*
flaxseed	grapeseed oil
walnut oil	peanut oil
	cottonseed oil
	borage oil*
	sesame oil
	primrose oil*

*These are healthful, despite being omega-6.

These simple tips will help you keep it all straight:

- Eat monounsaturated-rich foods, such as Australian macadamia nut oil when cooking and either macadamia nut oil or estate-bottled olive oil for cold uses.
- Consume more fatty fish, flaxseeds, and green leafy vegetables.
- Take a good omega-3 fatty-acid supplement.
- Avoid hydrogenated fats.
- Avoid oils high in omega-6: corn, safflower, sunflower, soybean, or cottonseed.
- Avoid trans-fats by cutting down on processed foods, deep-fried foods, and fast foods.
- Omega-3s = good; anti-inflammatory.
- Omega-6s = bad; pro-inflammatory.
- Maintain as close to a 1:1 ratio of omega-6 to omega-3 fatty acids as possible.

To help you keep this in perspective, here is another quick reference guide to the who's who of oils and fats.

Saturated Fats and Oils	Monounsaturated Oils	Polyunsaturated Oils
butter	macadamia nut oil	corn oil
coconut oil	olive oil	peanut oil
palm oil	high-oleic sunflower	sunflower oil
palm kernel oil	high-oleic safflower	safflower oil
animal fat	avocado oil	cottonseed oil
cocoa butter	canola oil	walnut oil
ghee		sesame oil
margarine		pumpkin seed oil
		grapeseed oil
		soybean oil
		primrose oil
		borage oil
		fish oils

Betty, a fifty-two-year-old client of mine, asked to be included in the patients' success stories because when she started this program, she never thought of how easy it would be to lose weight and reduce her menopausal symptoms. She had tried to lose the same twenty-five pounds since age forty-five and had failed with every new diet. At fifty, she began to experience severe hot flashes, memory loss, and mood swings as she entered menopause. And, of course, Betty couldn't lose weight, although she had tried everything from starvation to Atkins. Yet in her first two weeks on the Hamptons Diet, she lost seven pounds, and after the first month her hot flashes diminished to less than one a day. "I know it's because I'm now monounsaturated-rich!" she said. After getting rid of all the packaged and boxed foods she was addicted to, she began to use Australian macadamia nut oil exclusively in her kitchen. She soon felt much better, and the weight just melted off.

To get the ball rolling, be like Betty and follow these guidelines to get the full benefit of the Hamptons Diet:

1. Monounsaturated fats are the best.

2. Don't eat any trans-fatty acids if you can avoid them.
   - Avoid processed foods.
   - Avoid any ingredients that list "partially hydrogenated" oils (the type of oil doesn't matter; the level of hydrogenation does).
   - Avoid margarine, vegetable shortenings, canola oil, and fast foods.
3. Some saturated fats are okay.
   - Choose lean meats over fatty meats.
   - Good medium-chain triglycerides are found here, so don't avoid these completely.
4. Eat more omega-3 fatty acids.
   - Increase your fish consumption.
   - Increase your consumption of flaxseeds, walnuts, almonds, macadamia nuts, and green leafy vegetables.
5. Eat much less omega-6 fatty acids.
   - Avoid oils that are high in omega-6 fatty acids, such as grape-seed, corn, safflower, sunflower, soybean, and cottonseed oils.
   - Decrease your consumption of processed foods.
6. Try to maintain a 1:1 balance of omega-6 to omega-3 fatty acids.
   - By doing everything recommended here and following the Hamptons Diet, you will be close to achieving an ideal nutrition program.
7. When choosing an oil, select one with a high smoke point, low levels of polyunsaturated omega-6 fats or the ideal 1:1 ratio of omega-6 to omega-3 fatty acids, and the highest levels of omega-9 monounsaturated oleic acid.

CHAPTER 6

The Hamptons Diet
Menu Plans

Joan came into my office because she was menopausal, thirty pounds overweight, and had been diabetic for the last three years. Joan was a Hollywood celebrity with a house in the Hamptons, who was known for her outrageous behavior. She had been a party girl in her youth— a trust-fund baby who started her own company, which is now worth millions. Everyone liked to see her at their parties because wherever she went, she always attracted the press, but many people would have preferred that she move out of the Hamptons. She was a rude neighbor. Joan wasn't certain she wanted to consult with me because she'd tried low-carbohydrate diets in the past, and they never really worked for her. A friend of hers convinced her that I would be able to help. Joan's friend knew that I had the secret weapon of Australian macadamia nut oil at my disposal and was keeping it to myself and my patients, before this book came out.

Joan had always managed to lose a few pounds on other low-carbohydrate diet approaches, and her blood sugar readings improved somewhat but never as much as she desired. So, I started Joan on my monounsaturated-rich, low-carbohydrate diet. In three months, she lost twenty-four pounds, at an average of two pounds per week. That's fairly significant for a woman in menopause and is more than she'd ever lost on any other low-carbohydrate plan.

In addition, her daily and her long-range blood sugar readings improved dramatically. She was able to cut her medication use in half. By the end of six months, Joan was off all diabetes medications, had normal blood sugar readings, had lost forty-five pounds, and, needless to say, was delighted. Her menopausal symptoms of hot flashes even improved. She accomplished all of this simply by following the Hamptons Diet program that I describe in this book and by "getting an oil change." She didn't even create her own variations, she liked the original diet menu that much.

Expectations

As I stated in my previous diet book, our expectations about weight loss always affect our results. If we don't lose as much as we want or expect to lose, it often gives us an excuse to go off our diet. Nevertheless, I'm including the following weight-loss projections because people just want to know.

So, the average weight loss for people who stick to the Hamptons Diet is 3 to 4 pounds per week for a man and 2 to 4 pounds per week for a woman. If you are extremely obese, you can expect to lose weight more quickly than this. If you have only a few pounds to lose, then expect to lose weight a little more slowly. These are only averages for people who have been on the Hamptons Diet. I've seen many clients lose weight a lot faster than this, as well as some who have lost weight more slowly. The important thing is to stick with the program and follow it as closely as you can. Even if you have a lot of weight to lose, 1 pound per week is the equivalent of 50 pounds in a year—something to be extremely proud of.

Weight-Loss Mechanics—It's as Easy as ABC

In the following chapters, I outline a program that's suitable for three different groups of people. A suggested menu is given, followed by recipes for each dish. The basic menu is the same for all three groups. Some groups are allowed more food—that is, more carbohydrates—and this will be clearly demarcated on the menu. For people who desire food items other than those on the menu, I list foods for each group that may be substituted. This means that any A food can be substituted for any other A food in the same category. The foods are further subdivided into classes of foods, such as proteins and carbohydrates, so that you'll know how to make the correct substitutions. I don't want you to go hungry at any meal. You'll have plenty of food to eat, and you should never skip meals. Skipping meals can make you hungrier at the next meal, causing you to eat more than you should, or hunger might tempt you to make improper decisions about the food you eat.

If you require more than thirty days to lose weight or if you still need more suggestions, simply use the provided food tables to replace the original menu items with other great meals. The level of monounsaturated fat in each group is consistent with what's necessary to achieve long-lasting health benefits.

How Much Weight Do I Really Need to Lose?

The beauty of the Hamptons Diet program is that I've done all the work for you. Achieving weight loss and good health can be really easy now. You no longer have to choose between one or the other. To figure out how much weight you need to lose, refer to a body mass index (BMI) chart, which you can find online or in a doctor's office. This index takes into account the health benefits of weight loss and is much more realistic than the old height/weight tables that I used to dread when I was overweight. Extremely muscular men and women will have higher BMIs and will still be healthy. The BMI is made for someone of average build. You can also figure this out by using the following formula and a calculator.

Three steps are involved in calculating your BMI:

1. Multiply your weight in pounds by 703.
2. Square your height in inches (e.g., 6 feet = 72 inches, so $72 \times 72 = 5,184$).
3. Divide the total arrived at in Step 1 by the total arrived at in Step 2.

That number is your body mass index or BMI.

The number you're shooting for is a BMI of somewhere between 20 and 25—higher for a man and lower for a woman, of course.

If you want to figure out an exact number, that's fine with me, but it's something I never do with patients. I think it's far more important to develop healthful eating habits that will stay with you for the rest of your life, rather than just reach your goal weight and go back to your nasty old eating habits, which prompted you to buy this book in the first place. A rule of thumb that I use is to find out what my patients' lowest and highest weights were and when these occurred. If your lowest weight was in college or after a very stressful time, then it's not realistic to expect to reach that weight ever again. The older you are, the higher your goal weight should be. If your lowest weight was just a few years ago and your weight gain is strictly due to bad eating habits, then you can expect to reach that number. Otherwise, I generally add 5 pounds to a woman's lowest weight ever and 8 to 10 pounds if she is postmenopausal. For a man, I add about 10 pounds to his lowest weight ever if he is older than fifty. If he is younger than fifty, I just add 5 pounds, and those are my goal weights. This holds true only for a person who was thin at some point in his or her life. Everyone's goal weight is different, and that's why I don't like to emphasize this point. My rule of thumb is just that and doesn't hold true for everyone—the previous calculation is the official measurement. If you have never been thin, then a good place to start is with the BMI calculation and give yourself a few pounds of wiggle room. This makes it easier on the psyche, too—a very important part of the dieting equation and one that I don't address in this book, but I do in *Thin For Good*.

Where Do *I* Begin?

It's really easy to figure out where to begin with the Hamptons Diet. This is probably the only place in the world where you want to leave the A list behind. If you have

- More than 10 pounds to lose, start with the A diet.
- Less than 10 pounds or are within 5 to 10 pounds of your goal weight, start with the B diet.
- Been through the Hamptons Diet plan and have already

followed the A, the B, or both, or you just want to be healthy and are thin enough, start with the C diet.

The A List

This is not a statement about your social standing. It is the place where most people will start on the diet program. Group A suggestions are for those of you who need to lose more than ten pounds. You may include all the foods outlined in Group A suggestions and should keep your carbohydrate count below 30 grams per day. Follow this rule for as many weeks as it takes to get close to your goal weight. Being close to your goal weight will be different for everyone, but I define close as five to ten pounds away from your goal: less for people who have less to lose and more for people who have a lot to lose. Once you have gotten close to your goal weight, then move on to group B.

The B List: The Transitional Phase

Group B suggestions are for people who need to lose less than ten pounds or for those who are nearing their goal weight. For people who started in Group A, Group B is a transitional-stage diet program. Most people in this group will need to keep their daily carbohydrate count anywhere between 40 and 60 grams—less for women. Once you have achieved your goal weight, simply begin to follow the menu suggestions for people in Group C. In other words, eat the food suggested in Group A, plus you can add the foods suggested for group B to your diet. You don't have to eat the entire suggested menu on any given day, but you may.

The C List: Maintenance and Health Phase

Group C suggestions are for people who don't need to lose any weight but want to do the Hamptons Diet simply because of its health benefits or because everyone they know is doing it. No matter what your reason, this phase can also be considered the maintenance part of the program for people who started the Hamptons Diet in either Groups A or B. To follow this menu regime, simply eat the foods in Group A and add on the foods listed for Group B or C and, in some cases, both. This will give you a good idea of the carbohydrate count needed for healthful living. The daily carbohydrate count is approximately 55 to 65 grams for women and 65 to 85 grams for men.

Carbohydrate Count Adjustments

Your actual carbohydrate intake will have to be adjusted to fit your lifestyle and your metabolism. I'm not able to tell you exactly how many carbohydrates you can eat every day to maintain your weight. Some people may be able to eat a little bit more than suggested, and others will have to eat less than suggested. You'll have to make those adjustments at home without my guidance. However, I can advise you of the healthful carbohydrates to eat, and this is where the Hamptons Diet Pyramids come into play. They will provide you with the information you need to lead a healthful, monounsaturated-rich lifestyle, while still maintaining the terrific weight loss you worked so hard for.

Once you reach the maintenance phase and start to incorporate more foods and more carbohydrates into your diet, if your weight begins to creep upward, there are two things you can do. The first is to increase your level of exercise. The second is to lower your carbohydrate level to the point where you weren't gaining weight. Then, increase the carbohydrate level more slowly and try again. Or, you can try increasing the carbohydrates on just a few days each week, slowly adding carbohydrates that way. There are dozens of ways to increase your carbohydrate level. You have to find the balance that works for you. But please follow one cardinal rule: Don't go back to the way you used to eat. It didn't work for you then, and it won't work for you now. Make permanent, healthful, and monounsaturated-rich changes. Live the Hamptons lifestyle, even if you don't like the beach.

The optimum monounsaturated-fat content of the diet is completely achieved if you simply use macadamia nut oil for all your cooking needs, regardless of the phase or the group you are in. The trick to the Hamptons Diet is to ensure not only that you eat fewer carbohydrates, but that the carbohydrates you eat are healthful and the fats you consume are mostly monounsaturated. Eating healthful good fats and cutting down on your consumption of sugar and simple carbohydrates significantly decreases your risk of developing many types of disease and gives you lots of energy to boot. By the time you reach the C list, your health will have improved, and you'll be able to estimate the level of carbohydrates that's necessary to maintain your weight.

Another secret of the Hamptons Diet: it takes advantage of the little known thermic effect of food, or TEF. Approximately 10 percent of your body's calorie consumption is related to TEF. The minimally processed foods, either raw or slightly cooked vegetables, and the fiber-rich whole grains and fruits rich espoused by this eating plan place a greater digestive demand on your body, thereby potentially increasing your metabolism and the number of calories burned as your body processes what you eat.

Menu Plans

The numbers listed after each menu item are the approximate grams of carbohydrates it contains. Just add the number of carbohydrates for every item you eat, to know the total in each meal. This will also help you determine your maintenance level of carbohydrate grams.

Day 1

BREAKFAST

Goat Cheese and Arugula Omelet, 4

B: 4 ounces of cottage cheese, 8

C: ½ of whole wheat bagel, 14

LUNCH

Roast Beef with Melted Provolone Roll-Ups, 2

Green salad with choice of dressing, 4

B/C: 1 small tangerine, 9

DINNER

Creole Rubbed Tuna Steak, 1

Gardiner's Zucchini Salad, 6

½ cup raspberries with crème fraiche, 6

C: Vegetable Medley à la Noyack, 8

SNACK

Green and red pepper strips with your choice of dipping sauce, 3

Total carbohydrates per day for A = 23–26
Total carbohydrates per day for B = 40–43
Total carbohydrates per day for C = 62–65

Day 2

BREAKFAST

Big Benedict with Chipotle Hollandaise, 5

C: Served over 1 slice whole grain toast, 12

LUNCH

Acabonac Cheesecake, 6

Small green salad with choice of dressing, 4

B/C: ½ orange, 8

DINNER

Caesar Salad, 4

Mill Creek Lobster, 2

Rose Hill Collard Greens, 4

B/C: 1 small peach, 9

C: ½ cup steamed curried brown rice, 18

SNACK

1 ounce of macadamia nuts, 4

Total carbohydrates per day for A = 27–29
Total carbohydrates per day for B = 44–46
Total carbohydrates per day for C = 74–76

Day 3

BREAKFAST

Ricotta Macadamia Nut Muffins, 4

LUNCH

Egg Salad Maconnaise, 0

B: Served on two Wasa Crisp crackers, 6

C: On two slices of whole rye bread, 24

DINNER

Hayground Grilled Steak with Chipotle and Bacon, 2

Etruscan Spinach, 4

B/C: 1 small apricot, 6

C: ½ small baked sweet potato with butter or drizzled
macadamia nut oil, 10

SNACK

Celery sticks with one of the dipping sauces, 2

Total carbohydrates per day for A = 10–12
Total carbohydrates per day for B = 22–24
Total carbohydrates per day for C = 56–58

Day 4

BREAKFAST

Farmers' Market Salad, 6

LUNCH

Stuffed Burgers à la Halsey, 1

Small mesclun salad with choice of dressing, 2

B/C: ½ cup of cantaloupe, 7

DINNER

Cross Grilled Pork Chops with Pico de Gallo, 3

Three Mile Asparagus, 4

B: ½ serving of Macadamiaotash, 10

C: Full serving of Macadamiaotash, 20

Raspberry Cheesecake Square, 2

SNACK

Radishes with 2 ounces of cream cheese, 4

Total carbohydrates per day for A = 18–22
Total carbohydrates per day for B = 33–37
Total carbohydrates per day for C = 43–47

Day 5

BREAKFAST

Smoked salmon with 2 ounces of cream cheese, 2

B: Served on 1 Wasa Crisp cracker, 3

C: Served on 1 slice of toasted whole grain bread, 12

LUNCH

Lower East Side Guacamole, 5

B/C: 1 small plum, 7

DINNER

Settler's Stuffed Mushrooms, 4

Grilled Zucchini, 1

Arugula and Shaved Parmesan Salad with your choice of
dressing, 4

B: ½ peach, 8

C: Georgica Cheesecake with fresh raspberries, 8

SNACK

2 ounces of your choice of cheese, 2

Total carbohydrates per day for A = 16–18
Total carbohydrates per day for B = 34–36
Total carbohydrates per day for C = 54–56

Day 6

BREAKFAST

Scrambled Eggs with Sautéed Vegetables, 4

LUNCH

Turkey and Swiss Roll-Ups, 4

Small mixed green salad with choice of dressing, 4

C: Turkey and swiss on 2 slices of whole grain rye with mustard, 18

DINNER

Shad Roast on a Bed of Radish, Celery, and Fennel, 2

Chopped Salad, 4

B/C: Oven-Baked Mushroom Polenta, 14

C: ½ cup cantaloupe, 7

SNACK

Celery with 2 ounces of unsweetened nut butter, 4

Total carbohydrates per day for A = 18–22
Total carbohydrates per day for B = 32–36
Total carbohydrates per day for C = 57–61

Day 7

BREAKFAST

Decadent Dessert Almond Muffins, 7

These muffins are made from a specific mix especially for those on a reduced-sugar diet. They can be obtained through http://www. thesweetlifesweets.com. Just follow the recipe on the side of the can.

LUNCH

Tuna Salad Maconnaise, 1

B: Served on a Wasa Crisp, 3

C: Tuna Salad Maconnaise whole grain bread sandwich, 24

DINNER

Playhouse Snapper Stew, 6

Endive and Roquefort Salad, 4

Nutty Asparagus, 4

C: Serve over ½ cup Steamed Chipotle Quinoa, 20

B/C: ½ cup blueberries with whipped cream, 6

SNACK

1 ounce of almonds, 4

Total carbohydrates per day for A = 22–26
Total carbohydrates per day for B = 31–35
Total carbohydrates per day for C = 75–79

Day 8

BREAKFAST

Conscience Point Quiche, 6

C: 1 slice whole grain pumpernickel toast with no-sugar jelly, 14

LUNCH

Southwestern BLT, 2

B: ½ cup honeydew, 6

C: Southwestern BLT wrapped in whole wheat tortilla, 12

DINNER

Mecox Lamb Burgers, 3

Greek Salad, 4

Mohawk Spinach, 4

Ricotta Flan, 2

SNACK

2 ounces of spicy all-natural pepperoni, 0

Total carbohydrates per day for A = 21

Total carbohydrates per day for B = 27

Total carbohydrates per day for C = 53

Day 9

BREAKFAST

Soy Macadamia Nut Pancakes, 6

B/C: Soy Macadamia Nut Pancakes with Fresh Strawberry
    Topping, 2

LUNCH

Pecan Bacon Wrapped Pork Tenderloin, 1

Small green salad with your choice of dressing, 2

B/C: ½ cup sauerkraut, 5

DINNER

Flying Point Scallops with Bacon, 1

Mama's Stuffed Green Peppers, 6

Nutty Parmesan Salad, 4

B/C: ½ cup steamed brown rice with cloves, 18

Banana Cheesecake Square, 2

SNACK

1 hard-boiled egg, 1

Total carbohydrates per day for A = 22–23
Total carbohydrates per day for B = 47–48
Total carbohydrates per day for C = 47–48

Day 10

BREAKFAST

TexMex Tuna Melt, 2

B: Served over a Wasa Crisp cracker, 3

C: Served over a whole wheat English muffin, 12

LUNCH

Chihuahua Chicken Salad, 6

Small arugula salad with choice of dressing, 2

B/C: ½ apple, 12

DINNER

Flying Point Stuffed Cheeseburger, 4

Baked Eggplant Slices with Parmesan, 6

Sydneysider Salad, 4

C: ½ small sweet potato double baked with cheddar and bacon, 17

B/C: 2 Coconut Macadamiaroons, 10

SNACK

Zucchini sticks with choice of dip, 2

Total carbohydrates per day for A = 24–26
Total carbohydrates per day for B = 49–51
Total carbohydrates per day for C = 75–77

Day 11

BREAKFAST

Scrambled Eggs with Sausage and Scallions, 2

Corned Beef Hash, 5

LUNCH

Long Beach Shrimp Salad, 4

B (1 slice)/C (2 slices): Whole grain spelt toast points with salsa
    or pico de gallo, 12/24

C: ⅓ cup grapes, 5

DINNER

Fiery Escolar with Tabasco and Horseradish, 1

A/B: Steakhouse Wedge Salad, 2

C: Brown Rice and Chicken Salad, 18

B/C: Decadent Desserts Chocolate Bake Mix Brownie Recipe
    with Almonds, 7

Again, this can be found on the Web at http://www.
thesweetlifesweets.com, and with the recipe, simply add almonds
to the basic brownie recipe.

SNACK

1 ounce of walnuts, 4

Total carbohydrates per day for A = 14–18
Total carbohydrates per day for B = 33–37
Total carbohydrates per day for C = 66–70

Day 12

BREAKFAST

Bacon and Cheddar Omelet, 2

B: 1 Wasa Crisp, 3

C: 1 slice of whole grain spelt bread, 12

LUNCH

Mushroom-Filled Goat Cheese Burger, 3

B/C: Warm Coleslaw Salad, 8

B/C: ½ cup watermelon, 5

DINNER

Bayou Catfish with Vegetables and Basil Cream, 6

Caesar Salad, 4

C: ½ cup amaranth with basil flakes, 22

Blackberry Float, 6

SNACK

1 ounce of sunflower seeds, 4

Total carbohydrates per day for A = 23–25
Total carbohydrates per day for B = 40–42
Total carbohydrates per day for C = 70–72

Day 13

BREAKFAST

Quiche Florentine, 6

B/C: 1 small apricot, 5

LUNCH

North of the Highway Hot Dogs, 2

Cold Cauliflower Salad, 3

C: Fried Hot Dogs served in whole-grain hot dog roll, 12

DINNER

Beef Tenderloin with Provençal Maconnaise, 0

Smothered Belle Green Beans, 5

C: Mashed ½ sweet potato with scallion and garlic, 14

B/C: Mixed Berry Float, 6

SNACK

2 ounces of sliced turkey, 0

Total carbohydrates per day for A = 16
Total carbohydrates per day for B = 27
Total carbohydrates per day for C = 53

Day 14

BREAKFAST

Laredo Baked Eggs, 4

C: Served with 1 slice of whole rye toast and pico de gallo, 13

LUNCH

East Asian Chicken Soup, 3

Small romaine salad, with your choice of dressing, 4

B/C: 1 small peach, 9

DINNER

Halibut with Lemon and Coriander Oil, 0

Lemon Spinach, 4

B/C: Quinoa Constalliado, 25

C: 4 ounces of ricotta with cinnamon and Stevia or Splenda to taste, 4

SNACK

2 sticks of all-natural tuna jerky, 0

Total carbohydrates per day for A = 15
Total carbohydrates per day for B = 49
Total carbohydrates per day for C = 66

Day 15

BREAKFAST

Cabo Pork Posole, 4

C: Served with warm whole corn tortillas, 12

LUNCH

Roast Beef Rolls with Mustard Horseradish Cream à la Brent's, 7

C: Beef Rolls served open faced with 1 slice of whole grain bread, 12

B: 1 small apricot, 6

DINNER

Korean Spiced Fried Chicken, 0

Chinese Cabbage Coleslaw, 2

B/C: Sweet potato gratin, 18

1 small peach, 7

SNACK

2 ounces of sliced all-natural salami, 0

Total carbohydrates per day for A = 20
Total carbohydrates per day for B = 44
Total carbohydrates per day for C = 62

Day 16

BREAKFAST

Baked Eggs with 2 Cheeses, 4

B/C: 1 small plum, 8

LUNCH

Quogue Kebabs, 6

C: Served with ½ cup steamed brown rice with scallions, 16

B: Small radish and fennel salad, 4

DINNER

Tuscan Grilled Steak, 2

Neapolitan Cauliflower, 6

B/C: Small radicchio and endive salad with Roquefort dressing, 4

C: Whole Grains Pilaf, 15

SNACK

1 ounce of macadamia nuts, crushed with 2 ounces of cream
    cheese, 6

Total carbohydrates per day for A = 20–24
Total carbohydrates per day for B = 38–42
Total carbohydrates per day for C = 69–73

Day 17

BREAKFAST

Meier's Path Eggs, 2

B/C: Sweet potato home fries, 12

LUNCH

Backyard Steak Salad, 3

C: 1 small tangerine, 9

DINNER

Swordfish à la Woodsfield, 0

Hamptons Bay Beans, 4

B/C: Stone-ground corn fritters; 1 for B; 2 for C (14/28)

½ cup watermelon, 5

SNACK

1 ounce of walnuts, 4

Total carbohydrates per day for A = 14–18
Total carbohydrates per day for B = 40–44
Total carbohydrates per day for C = 63–67

Day 18

BREAKFAST

Ricotta Pignoli Muffins, 4

C: ⅓ cup pineapple, 6

LUNCH

Sayre's Path Broccoli Casserole, 7

Small green salad with your choice of dressing, 2

C: ½ orange, 8

DINNER

Spicy Grilled Steak, 0

Sesame Broccoli, 3

B/C: Southern Sophisticate Corn Pilaf, 15

½ cup cottage cheese with fresh raspberry sauce, 6

SNACK

Green and red pepper slices with 2 ounces unsweetened almond butter, 4

Total carbohydrates per day for A = 22–26
Total carbohydrates per day for B = 37–41
Total carbohydrates per day for C = 51–55

Day 19

BREAKFAST

Frittata with Queso Blanco and Peppers, 4

B/C: 1 small nectarine, 12

LUNCH

Bacon Lettuce Turkey Twist, 2

C: Bacon Lettuce Turkey Twist served on 1 slice of whole grain toast, 14

B: Tomato and cucumber salad, 6

DINNER

Daddy's Meatballs, 2

Stuffed Zucchini Sedona Style, 4

C: Mediterranean Couscous Salad, 25

A/B: Salad with toasted pine nuts, sheep's milk cheese, and warm creamy Italian dressing, 4

B/C: ½ cup blueberries with whipped cream, 6

SNACK

2 ounces of St. Andre cheese on 1 Wasa Crisp, 5

Total carbohydrates per day for A = 16–21
Total carbohydrates per day for B = 40–45
Total carbohydrates per day for C = 69–74

Day 20

BREAKFAST

Asparagus with Buffalo Mozzarella, 4

B/C: Strawberry Breakfast Smoothie, 6

LUNCH

Artichoke Shrimp Chowder, 8

Small mesclun salad with your choice of dressing, 2

DINNER

Milanese Shrimp, 1

Dressy Spring Salad, 5

B/C: North Haven Lentil Salad, 12

C: Brussels Sprouts Amandine, 4

Coconut Crème Pie, 4

SNACK

1 hard-boiled egg, 1

Total carbohydrates per day for A = 24–25
Total carbohydrates per day for B = 40–41
Total carbohydrates per day for C = 44–45

Day 21

BREAKFAST

Frittata with Zucchini and Mushroom, 3

B/C: 1 Wasa Crisp, 3

LUNCH

Hedges Lane Ham Casserole, 7

B: ½ medium grapefruit, 9

DINNER

Chicken Breast Pescatore, 1

West Hampton Eggplant Vinaigrette, 6

Chicory salad with Italian dressing, 4

C: ½ cup cooked kasha with fresh basil, 22

B: ½ baked sweet potato with butter and fines herbes, 14

C: ½ cup mixed berries with crème fraiche, 6

SNACK

2 ounces of Chinese snow pea pods, flash fried and
salted, 4

Total carbohydrates per day for A = 21–25
Total carbohydrates per day for B = 47–51
Total carbohydrates per day for C = 62–66

Day 22

BREAKFAST

2 poached eggs over spinach, 3

B: 1 Wasa Crisp, 3

C: ½ whole grain English muffin, 14

LUNCH

Chicken Salad Maconnaise, 0

C: 1 slice whole grain pumpernickel, 12

B/C: 1 small peach, 9

DINNER

Kobe Short Ribs, 2

Thai-Style Stir Fried Vegetables, 4

B/C: ½ cup brown rice with Chinese spices, 17

Key Lime Cheesecake Squares, 4

SNACK

1 ounce of mixed nuts, 4

Total carbohydrates per day for A = 13–17
Total carbohydrates per day for B = 42–46
Total carbohydrates per day for C = 68–72

Day 23

BREAKFAST

Soy Pecan Pancakes, 6

B/C: Served with fresh blueberry topping and whipped cream, 6

LUNCH

Cold Devon Asparagus Soup with Lemon Crème Fraiche, 6

B/C: ½ cup watermelon, 5

DINNER

White Sands Pork Shoulder, 1

Chilled Laotian Asparagus, 3

Simple green salad with Bacon and Roquefort Dressing, 4

B/C: Baked Summer Farm Fresh Vegetables, 8

C: ½ cup herbed brown rice, 18

SNACK

2 ounces of sliced roast beef, 0

Total carbohydrates per day for A = 20
Total carbohydrates per day for B = 39
Total carbohydrates per day for C = 57

Day 24

BREAKFAST

Hotel California Omelet with Guacamole, 4

B/C: Sweet potato fries and onions, 15

LUNCH

Rosemary Grilled Flanken, 0

Summer Salad with Fresh Herbs, 2

C: 1 small plum, 8

DINNER

Wain's Rack of Lamb, 1

Green Beans with Lemon, 3

B/C: Tabbouleh Salad, 20

Georgica Cheesecake with Fresh Boysenberry Topping, 8

SNACK

2 cheddar cheese sticks, 2

Total carbohydrates per day for A = 18–20
Total carbohydrates per day for B = 53–55
Total carbohydrates per day for C = 61–63

Day 25

BREAKFAST

Almond Coconut Muffins, 9

These are the Decadent Dessert Muffins; simply add unsweetened coconut to the basic muffin recipe.

LUNCH

Settler's Asparagus, 5

B: ½ cup watermelon, 5

C: 1 orange, 14

DINNER

Curried Beef, 0

Creole Marinated Vegetables, 6

Warm Braised Spinach Salad with Pecans, 4

B/C: ½ Double-Baked Sweet Potato with Cheddar and Bacon, 16

B/C: Mixed Berry Float, 6

SNACK

Cucumber and zucchini slices with 2 ounces of St. Andre cheese, 3

Total carbohydrates per day for A = 24–27
Total carbohydrates per day for B = 51–54
Total carbohydrates per day for C = 65–68

Day 26

BREAKFAST

Atlantic Beach Avocado Boats, 8

C: 1 slice of whole grain wheat toast, 12

LUNCH

South Hampton Scallops Provençal, 4

B: 1 Wasa Crisp, 3

C: 1 small nectarine, 13

DINNER

Chicken Devon, 1

Job's Okra, 5

Spinach and arugula salad, 2

B/C: ½ cup herbed brown rice, 18

B/C: Lemon Cream Ice, 6

SNACK

1 ounce of macadamia nuts, 4

Total carbohydrates per day for A = 20–24
Total carbohydrates per day for B = 47–51
Total carbohydrates per day for C = 72–76

Day 27

BREAKFAST

Wainscott Torte, 6

B/C: Breakfast Smoothie with Peanut Butter, 6

LUNCH

Town Line Eggs, 6

Small green salad with your choice of salad dressing, 4

DINNER

Montauk Shrimps in Gansett Green Sauce, 3

Sautéed kale and collard greens, 4

B: 1 small plum, 8

C: ½ cup ricotta cheese with cinnamon, 6

C: ½ cup cilantro brown rice, 18

SNACK

Celery sticks with 1 ounce of cashew butter, 6

Total carbohydrates per day for A = 23–29
Total carbohydrates per day for B = 37–43
Total carbohydrates per day for C = 61–67

Day 28

BREAKFAST

Greens Frittata, 4

B: 1 Wasa Crisp with almond butter, 3

C: 1 slice of whole grain rye with butter, 12

LUNCH

Northwest Smoked Pork, 0

Small green salad with your choice of dressing, 2

C: Smoked Pork on 1 slice of whole grain bread, 12

B: 1 small plum, 8

DINNER

Down-Home Brisket with Texas Pecan Cilantro Pesto, 3

Cauliflower au gratin, 5

Southwestern Chinese Cabbage Coleslaw, 2

B: Southern Succotash, 4

C: ⅓ cup whole wheat pasta with garlic and red pepper, 16

B/C: ½ cup raspberries with whipped cream, 6

SNACK

Slices of all-natural pepperoni, 0

Total carbohydrates per day for A = 16
Total carbohydrates per day for B = 37
Total carbohydrates per day for C = 65

Day 29

BREAKFAST

2 poached eggs with bacon, 2

B: ½ medium grapefruit, 6

C: Served over ½ whole wheat English muffin, 14

LUNCH

Sag Taco Salad, 5

C: Served in a taco shell, 16

DINNER

Abraham's Curried Chicken, 4

Roasted Asparagus with Shallots, 4

Caesar Salad, 4

B/C: ½ cup brown rice with cumin, 18

Coconut Cream Pie Ice, 6

SNACK

2 ounces of your favorite cheese, 4

Total carbohydrates per day for A = 20–24
Total carbohydrates per day for B = 44–48
Total carbohydrates per day for C = 74–78

Day 30

BREAKFAST

Salmon Melts, 1

B: Melted onto a Wasa Crisp, 3

C: Melted onto 1 slice of whole grain rye bread, 12

LUNCH

Peconica Dogs, 4

Small salad with your choice of dressing, 4

C: 1 small peach, 9

C: Served on a whole grain hot corn tortilla, 11

DINNER

    Simple Roast Chicken with Fresh Herbs and Butter, 0

    Broccoli with Hollandaise Sauce, 6

    Frisee salad with choice of dressing, 2

    B/C: Mashed sweet potatoes with butter and garlic, 24

    Orange Cheesecake Squares, 2

SNACK

    2 ounces turkey slices, 0

Total carbohydrates per day for A = 19

Total carbohydrates per day for B = 46

Total carbohydrates per day for C = 66

I hope these menu plans are making your mouth water as much as mine did while I was creating them. I think there's a good mixture of simple after-work dishes, along with recipes that require a little more preparation and time in the kitchen. So, no matter what your lifestyle, something on this menu plan should suit you. Also, the daily menus incorporate many different regional cuisines, so that you won't become bored with eating this new healthy way.

For each dish mentioned, there is an accompanying recipe. For certain foods, though, no recipe is given; for example, green salads. I assume that everyone knows how to clean and prepare lettuce for a salad. You will, however, find many unique salad and vegetable dressing recipes that feature the delicious and slightly nutty taste of premium macadamia nut oil.

For other recipes that may be variations on a theme, I simply listed them as variations of the first recipe, so you should be able to find what you're looking for quite easily.

Another tasty surprise is that some of the recipes in this book were created by well-known celebrity chefs. These recipes will be indicated, and short biographies of the two chefs appear in this book's resource section. The first chef is Thomas Valenti, who is the owner of Ouest and 'Cesca in New York City. Tom helped to pioneer the interest in Australian macadamia nut oil and introduced it to many chefs and consumers. The other chef is Douglas Rodriguez, who owns Ola in New York City and Alma de Cuba in Philadelphia. Doug is a dedi-cated low-carbohydrate and monounsaturated-fat enthusiast. He has lost weight himself by lowering his carbohydrate consumption. I con-sider them both dear friends and am thrilled that they are helping you discover that low-carbohydrate and monounsaturated-rich cooking doesn't have to be dull. In fact, it is quite gourmet.

Jamie, a forty-eight-year-old mother of three, had gradually, with each successive pregnancy, gained forty-five pounds over the years. Other than the weight, her only other health complaint was fatigue, which she attributed to raising three kids while running her own busi-ness. Jamie prepared expensive summer homes for their rental guests and owners. If this diet worked, she wanted to put this book in each home's gift basket. She had tried other low-carbohydrate diets in the past but always got really bored after about two weeks. After all, how much bacon and eggs could one eat?

I often heard this common refrain in my office. It always left me feeling a little confused because I hardly ever ate eggs in the morning, simply because I didn't have time to cook them, except on the week-ends. I explained to Jamie that she had an abundance of foods to choose from. She just had to get out of her rut and explore the super-market a little more.

Jamie was skeptical when I suggested this. But I asked her to ded-icate one weekday evening or one weekend day to the task and to slowly go through the supermarket, exploring its shelves. I love to do this. I usually do it when I travel because the foods are more exotic, but I also explore my regular grocery store at least once a month. In fact, I did it yesterday. Although, I must admit, I was preparing the recipes and the menus for this book, so I needed to be creative. That's how I justified the time expenditure. Jamie hesitantly agreed to try my suggestion, because she really wanted to drop the weight this time. Her oldest son was also starting to gain weight, and she wanted to set a good example for him.

Two weeks later, Jamie triumphantly returned to my office with a list of forty new foods that she hadn't even known existed prior to our last visit. In fact, she was so excited that she helped me compile the lists in this chapter. And, she lost fifty pounds and has kept them off for the last three years.

Since the issue of boredom is a recurring one in my office, Jamie and I put together the following lists so that people could see that they have an amazing assortment of foods to choose from, without resorting to simple carbohydrates in order to fill up. Besides, why do we still think we have to fill up at every meal? That's the way an overweight person thinks. Start thinking like a thin person: Eat only when hungry; eat what is there; and most important, stop eating before you are full. It takes about twenty minutes for your brain to register that you're full. If you eat until you're full, you have eaten too much. Stop eating just before you feel full and see if that helps with the process. I know it helps me. This is also a great tip for those in the maintenance phase of the Hamptons Diet.

The lists of foods are not meant to be exhaustive, although I did try to make them complete. Since the possibilities are endless, I could have dedicated months of research to finding all the foods that a person could possibly eat, yet I still would have missed some. These lists contain the most popular foods that we eat. If I missed anything, kindly write to me and let me know, so that I can add it to future editions.

There are three different lists: A, B, and C. For the most part, any item in List A can be substituted for any other item of the same kind in the menu plans. This not only gives you the opportunity to create many more meals from the menu plans but allows people to substitute things they prefer for each menu item. The same holds true for any item in the other two lists. List B foods can substitute for any of the B suggestions in the menu plan, and List C foods can substitute for any of the C suggestions in the menu plan.

Each group will have a subset within it that contains protein, complex carbohydrates (further divided into grains and vegetables), and fruits. Again, among the groups, each protein can substitute for a protein, each fruit for a fruit, and each complex carbohydrate for a complex carbohydrate.

List A

Proteins

almonds	bacon bits*	beef jerky—check
anchovy	bass	the sugar content
bacon—not sugar	beef	beefalo
cured		

blood sausage
bluefish
bockwurst
bologna*
bonito
brains
bratwurst
burbot
butterfish
Canadian bacon
capocollo
carp
catfish
caviar
cheese, including but
  not limited to:
  Asiago
  Babybel
  Bel Paese
  Brie
  Camembert
  cheddar
  colby
  colby jack
  cottage cheese
  cream cheese
  edam
  farmer's cheese
  feta
  fontina
  goat milk cheeses
  Gouda
  Gruyere
  Havarti
  Jarlsberg
  Limburger

Mascarpone
Monterey Jack
mozzarella
Muenster
Neufchatel
Parmesan
pecorino
Port Salut
pot cheese
provolone
Queso Blanco
ricotta
Romano
Roquefort
St. Andre
string
swiss
taleggio
chicken
chitterlings, pork
clams
cod
corned beef
cornish game hens
crab
crayfish
cusk
cuttlefish
dolphin
drum
duck
eel
eggs
escolar
flatfish
flounder

frankfurter
frog's legs
gefilte fish
goat
goose
grouper
guinea hen
haddock
hake
halibut
ham, fresh
head cheese
herring
kidneys
kielbasa
knockwurst
lamb
ling
lingcod
lobster
mackerel
mahi-mahi
milkfish
monkfish
mortadella
mullet
ocean perch
octopus
opossum
orange roughy
pancreas
pastrami
pate
pepperoni
perch
pheasant

pigs feet
pigs knuckles
pike
pompano
pork
pork skins
pout
prosciutto
quail
rabbit
red snapper
redfish
roast beef—coldcut
rockfish
sablefish
salami
sardines
sausage—not sugar
   cured
scallops

scrod
scrup
sea bass
sea snail (whelk)
sea trout
shad
shark
sheepshead
shrimp
smelt
snapper
sole
spiny lobster
spot
squab
stomach
sturgeon
sucker
summer sausage
sunfish

swordfish
Taramosalata
thymus
tilefish
tofu
tongue
trout
tuna
turbot
turkey
veal
vegetarian bacon*
venison
Vienna sausage
whitefish
whiting
wild boar
wolf fish
yellowtail

Complex Carbohydrates—Vegetables

artichoke hearts—
   ½ cup
arugula
asparagus
avocado
bamboo shoots
basil
beet greens
Bibb lettuce
bok choy

Boston lettuce
broccoli
brussels sprouts
butterbur
capers
cauliflower
celery
celtus
cherry pepper
chicory

chicory greens
chile pepper
chives
cilantro
coconut
coconut milk
coconut water
collards
coriander
cos lettuce

*a soy- or vegetable-derived substitute

crookneck squash
cucumber
dandelion greens
dill
endive
escarole
garlic
green pepper
guacamole
horseradish
iceberg
jalapeno pepper
kohlrabi
mushrooms
mustard greens
mustard spinach

New England
  spinach
okra
olives
parsley
parsley root
piccalilli
radicchio
radish
red pepper
romaine
seaweed, raw
sesbania flower
shallots
spinach
sprouts

sunburst squash
swamp cabbage
swiss chard
taro leaf
taro shoots
tomatillo
turnips
turnip greens
watercress
wax beans
wax gourd
winged bean
yard-long beans
zucchini

Fruits

acerola
balsam pear
bitter melon
blackberries

blueberries
boysenberries
cantaloupe
raspberries

strawberries
watermelon

Spices

alfalfa seeds
anise seeds
basil
black pepper
caraway seeds
cardamom
cayenne pepper

celery seed
chervil
chili powder
cinnamon
cloves
clove seeds
cumin

dill seed
fennel seed
fenugreek seed
garam masala
garlic powder
garlic salt
ground ginger

habanero chili	nutmeg	rosemary
herbes de Provence	onion powder	saffron
kelp powder	onion salt	sage
lemon pepper	oregano	star anise
lemon thyme	oriental five spice	tarragon
mace	paprika	thyme
marjoram	poultry seasoning	turmeric
mustard (dry)	radish seeds	wasabi

Nuts and Nut Butters

almonds	macadamia nut	pumpkin seeds
Brazil nuts	pecans	walnuts
filberts	pine nuts	white sesame seeds

Miscellaneous

gelatin	mayonnaise	sour cream
heavy cream	mustard	vinegar
horseradish	pure distilled liquors	

List B

Proteins

abalone	oysters	squid
liver	seaweed (raw)	vegetable protein
mussels	soy protein	

Complex Carbohydrates—Vegetables

broad beans	carrots	cow-eyed peas
burdock root	celeriac	(black-eyed)
butternut squash	chayote	eggplant
cabbage	chicory root	fennel

ginger
gourd
green beans
green onion
Hubbard squash
hyacinth beans
kale
leek
lima beans

mung beans
onion
pickles
purslane
red cabbage
rhubarb
sauerkraut
savoy cabbage
scallop squash

shellie bean
snow peas
snow pea pods
sweet peppers
water chestnut
yam
yellow beans

Complex Carbohydrates—Grains

amaranth
brown rice
brown rice cereal
corn chips
farro
millet
oats

oat bran
oat meal—not
    instant
postum
puffed millet
puffed rice
puffed wheat

quinoa
sesame flour
spelt
tabbouleh
teff
wheat bran

Nuts and Nut Butters

cashews
hazelnuts

peanuts
pistachios

sesame seeds
sunflower seeds

Fruits

Apple—½
apricot
Asian pear
casaba melon
grapefruit
grapes
honeydew

kumquat
lemon
lime
loquat
mulberry
nectarine
peach

pineapple—½ cup
plum
prickly pear
sour cherries
tangerine
tomatillo
tomato

Miscellaneous

cocoa powder	seitan

Spices

cream of tartar	gumbo file	pumpkin pie spice
curry powder		

List C

Proteins

All animal proteins and most vegetable proteins should be on one of the other two lists.

Complex Carbohydrates—Vegetables and Legumes

acorn squash	great northern beans	pigeon beans
adzuki beans	Jerusalem artichoke	pinto beans
anasazi beans	jicama	plantain
baked beans	kidney beans	pumpkin
beets	lentils	red beans
black beans	lotus root	red kidney beans
breadfruit	miso	rutabaga
cassava (yucca)	moth bean	soybeans
chick peas	natto	split peas
christophene	navy beans	sweet potato
corn	parsnip	taro
dasheen (taro)	peas	white beans
feijoa	picante beans	yucca

Complex Carbohydrates—Grains

barley	brown rice	couscous
barley flakes	buckwheat	cracked whole wheat
barley flour	buckwheat groats	kamut
blue corn meal	bulgur wheat	kashi

oats	soy flour	wheat flakes
oat bran	steel-cut oats	whole farina
rolled oats	teff	whole wheat flour

Fruits

cherries	kiwi	red banana
guava	passion fruit	soursop
jackfruit	pear	yellow banana
kiwano	pomegranate	

Miscellaneous

| tahini (sesame paste) | tempeh | unsweetened yogurt |

Of course, I could not possibly name every food on the planet. So, if the food is not listed in any of the previous categories, simply try to find out its carbohydrate content. If it's below 10 grams per serving, it goes in List A; if it's between 10 and 30 grams per serving, it goes in List B; and if the food contains more than 30 grams per serving, it belongs in List C. Please keep in mind that these rules are for complex carbohydrates, not for sugar grams. Sugar grams are to be avoided at all times, especially while trying to lose weight. For those of you who are at your goal or are getting monounsaturated-rich for the health benefits, then limit sugar to special occasions. The easy thing to remember is that if the food didn't make this list, it should be avoided for either weight loss or health reasons.

Drinks

Another category of foods that I didn't mention is drinks. Beer and wine are prohibited, except on rare occasions for the List C group. Alcoholic drinks should be limited to pure distilled alcohols of your choosing: men are allowed 1.5 ounces of spirits 4 times per week and women, twice per week. Everything else you drink should be water, flavored seltzers, or any other soft drink that doesn't have carbohydrates. The one diet drink that I must caution against is Crystal Light. In my experience, and this is purely anecdotal, people who drank this lost weight more slowly than those who didn't. For health reasons, the less aspartame you consume, the better off you are.

Whole Grains: The Nicer Carbohydrate

Carbohydrates have taken a beating in the media lately, and rightly so. I feel that they have caused the horrible obesity epidemic we now face. They are responsible for increasing cholesterol levels, fostering heart disease, and dramatically increasing diabetes rates. However, not all carbohydrates are unhealthful. Simple carbohydrates are unhealthful and should come with a bigger warning than that found on cigarette packages. Many complex carbohydrates can be quite good for a balanced, healthful diet—the sine qua non of the Hamptons Diet.

Whole grains contain the bran (the outer layer), the endosperm (the starchy heart that's low in nutrients), and the germ (the internal embryo). They contain indigestible fiber, minerals, 10 to 15 percent protein by weight, and phytochemicals, such as phytic acid, phenolic compounds, amylase inhibitors, and saponins. These are found naturally in all grain products. When grains are refined, the bran, the germ, and all the healthful nutrients, including antioxidants, are removed.

According to the Iowa women's health study, Dr. David Jacobs and his colleagues found that women who ate at least one serving of whole-grain foods per day had a significantly lower rate of death from all causes when compared with women who ate almost no grains. In that same study, it was shown that whole-grain intake is directly related to a decreased risk of coronary heart disease.

Because whole grains cause only small rises in blood sugar and insulin release, whole grains in the right amounts may be beneficial in the diets of those with type II diabetes. Multiple studies show that people who eat more complex carbohydrates have a decreased risk for getting type II diabetes.

I'm not suggesting a diet that's rich in these types of foods. Rather, I do suggest a diet that incorporates complex carbohydrates because of their health benefits. You should stay away from any low-carbohydrate diet that encourages you to ignore these foods for the rest of your life. Most of the popular low-carbohydrate diets simply tell you to avoid carbs and eat all the protein you want. This is a bad message to send to an overweight person. Overweight people need to learn that part of a healthful, lifelong nutritional lifestyle program must include portion control. There can be no other way. My approach has always differed from Atkins's in this simple message: You can't eat all you want of anything and be healthy and thin for the rest of your life. It just doesn't work. Maintaining your weight loss is the hardest part of any dietary program, and the Hamptons Diet provides you with the tools you need to be successful.

Complex carbohydrates are an important part of the diet, as long as they're consumed in limited quantities. But we must avoid the type that we've grown accustomed to eating: simple sugar and simple carbohydrates.

Losing Weight

There you have it—a thirty-day meal plan that will change your life. Many of my patients have lost up to fourteen pounds in the first two weeks. When I told you the amount of weight you could expect to lose, I averaged out the weight loss over time. You'll lose the most in the beginning, then your weight loss will slow down. That's normal, so don't be discouraged. Your weight loss will not slow down and reach a plateau, as often happens with so many other low-carbohydrate diet programs.

Harriet went from size 22 to size 14 in four months on this program. She was skeptical of my claim that she wouldn't plateau. She had reached a plateau on every other diet she tried, and she'd been dieting most of her life. As is typical for women, she lost ten pounds in the first two weeks. When I saw her, she was pleased but still reluctant to admit that I was right. After one more month, her weight loss had slowed to two pounds per week, and Harriet told me that she was expecting it to stop at any minute. By the fourth month, I saw Harriet and she still continued to lose weight. She was the smallest she'd ever been since her teenage years—size 14. She was still losing weight, had not hit a plateau, and was overjoyed. At the time this book went to press, Harriet was a size 10 and said to please tell my readers that "this is the best diet I've ever been on in my life and that Australian macadamia nut oil is so delicious—I love it."

All of you now have the same information that Harriet had when she left my office. Follow the meal plans, use macadamia nut oil as your only oil source, and you'll lose weight and feel terrific. Be sure to have a good time along the way, and tell all your friends. Before we get to the recipes, you need to know a few more things.

CHAPTER 7

The Hamptons Diet
Supplement Plan

Henry started on the Hamptons Diet after receiving a very bad blood report from his primary-care physician. Henry wasn't used to things not going his way. He was a very successful record producer, a mogul—and he always got what he wanted. He led the good life and as a result was forty pounds overweight. His fasting blood sugar was slightly elevated at 115, his triglyceride level was 270, and his HDL (good) cholesterol was only 37 out of a total of 244. One of Henry's golfing buddies, a patient of mine, always raved about how much weight he'd lost, how easy it was, and how much his blood work had improved, so Henry decided to give me a call. I started him on the Hamptons dietary program, explained the importance of nutritional supplements, and turned him loose. He really didn't want to take supplements because he didn't want to look stupid carrying them around. However, they are a necessary part of any healthful and weight-loss lifestyle.

I simplified Henry's program and requested he take only the supplements that were most crucial for his weight loss. Within a week, Henry reported having a lot more energy. Within two weeks, he'd grown accustomed to taking the supplements and wouldn't even consider missing a dose. He attributed his improved health to their use. His vigor and well-being could also have been the result of his losing twelve pounds in those first two weeks. He could already fit into some of his old clothes, and everyone at the Maidstone, the most exclusive country club in the Hamptons, told him how great he looked and wanted to know what he was doing. He didn't want to talk about the program, though, until he was sure it would work. So, after two months, we drew some blood, and Henry was amazed at the results: a normal fasting blood sugar, thirty pounds lost, a cholesterol level of 199, with an HDL (good) of 55—an enormous improvement. These results may sound extraordinary, but they really aren't. To me, they're commonplace and what I expect. If a major improvement does not occur, I have to wonder what either I or the patient did wrong.

The Hamptons Diet Nutritional Supplement Protocol

I'll specify which supplements I consider necessary for the Hamptons Diet and then will include others that you may want to add or try because you have probably heard about them. I'll also list others that I would never recommend, so you'll know which ones to avoid. Of course, it's possible to lose weight on the Hamptons Diet without taking nutritional supplements. But my patients have told me that certain supplements really help, and I think they do, too, so I'm simply outlining my recommended program as if you were here in my office.

I think everyone who is dieting should take the following supplements. They'll help your weight loss, but they aren't wonder pills. They won't do anything if you don't follow the appropriate dietary regimen.

Essential Fatty Acids

These are the omega-3 and omega-6 fatty acids that I've discussed throughout this book. If you take nothing else, they are a crucial component of the Hamptons Diet protocol. I recommend supplementing with an omega-3 fish oil that contains eicosapentaenoic acid (EPA) and docosahexaenoic acid (DHA) in an approximately 3:2 ratio, for a total daily dosage of 1,500 mg, 500 mg three times per day, best taken with each meal. Many brands are on the market, so please get as close as possible to the dose I recommend. Also, when choosing a fish oil, make sure you buy a reputable brand from a company that tests its products for contaminants and mercury. These toxins accumulate in fish, so it's important that the ocean's pollutants be removed from your nutritional supplement. If you are a vegetarian and want to use flaxseed oil, that is second best, because flax contains more ALA than it does EPA and DHA.

Multivitamin

The multivitamin I recommend to patients is Life Force Multiple, created by a company named Source Naturals. It contains an extensive list of ingredients and is formulated to be a metabolic activator with components that work on the brain and nerves, the liver, heart and circulatory system, the immune system, and the musculoskeletal system. It is also a good source of antioxidants. Source Naturals' products are excellent; in appendix A, I list more of this company's outstanding products.

Chromium

This essential trace mineral was once found in our soil. Unfortunately, the soil has been so depleted, it's no longer available in any significant quantities and therefore must be taken as a supplement. Chromium is involved in the metabolism of insulin, in blood sugar regulation, and in fat metabolism. This mineral is essential for diabetics, as it has been shown to decrease blood sugar and decrease a patient's need for diabetic medication. Small amounts of chromium are also found in brewer's yeast, broccoli, some whole grains, cheese, mushrooms, and meat. As a supplement, it is available in the picolinate, the polynicotinate, and the GTF versions. More scientific evidence supports the use of the picolinate variety. The brand name that I like is a product that has been thoroughly researched, called Diachrome, which needs to be taken only once a day. But, if you don't use Diachrome, the dose of chromium should be 200 micrograms three times per day, taken with meals, for a total daily dose of 600 mg.

Carnitine

This is produced naturally in the body. It not only helps the body release fat for fuel during the weight-loss process but also provides up to two-thirds of the heart's daily energy requirements. It does this by transporting fats into the mitochondria, where they are burned for energy. Red meat is its largest source, with chicken, fish, eggs, and milk containing a much smaller amount. The recommended dose is 500 to 1,000 mg three times per day for a total daily dose of 1,500 to 3,000 mg. It is best taken on an empty stomach.

Coenzyme Q10

This is also naturally produced in the body and is universally found throughout the body. It is known to carry protons and electrons as the body burns energy, so it's essential in metabolism. It's not classified as a vitamin, a mineral, or an amino acid but is considered an antioxidant. It works in many different pathways in the body, especially in cardiac function, but for our purposes of weight loss, it can help facilitate the use of stored fat as fuel. The body's production of coenzyme Q10 peaks at age twenty, so it is essential to supplement this in most people. The best food sources are organ meats (liver and kidneys), other red meats, nuts, and unprocessed vegetable oils. Cereal, bran, and dark green vegetables will provide lesser amounts of this critical nutrient. Consuming it with oil or in an oil form helps it to be better absorbed. Also, you may want to take a B-complex supplement, as this is also a cofactor in the absorption of coenzyme Q10. The recommended dose is 100 mg, three times per day, taken with each meal, for a total daily dose of 300 mg.

Glutamine

This is the body's most abundant amino acid and has been shown to provide energy for the muscles. It's important in regulating many bodily functions. It does this by providing a nitrogen atom for synthesis into other amino acids and thus helps the body build proteins, glutathione, glucosamine, and vitamin B3, among others. I find that it helps people to handle sugar cravings, if they use it immediately when they crave something. Although it is abundant in many foods, you can never absorb the dosage you need unless you take supplements. As it helps to minimize sugar cravings, I recommend 500 mg three times per day (for a total of 1,500 mg) and as needed throughout the day when hungry. It is best taken on an empty stomach.

I recommend that each Hamptons dieter take the previous supplements, no matter which phase of the diet he or she is in. As your sugar cravings disappear, you probably won't need the glutamine. Other nutritional supplements currently on the market also tout weight loss as their major contribution. Since there are too many to elaborate on, I'll mention those that you may try if you'd like to because they are most likely not harmful to you, as well as those that you should avoid because I feel that they have some potential negative side effects.

Other Potentially Useful Supplements

Green Tea Extract

This is also known as *camellia sinensis.* As it is a plant extract, please ensure that what you're using contains at least 50 percent polyphenols in the form of EGCG catechins. These are the active ingredients; studies have shown that green tea extract works not by stimulating your metabolism and exciting you, as caffeine does, but by stimulating fat breakdown in your body. The recommended dose is around 300 mg three times a day with meals, for a total of 900 mg.

Choline

This is related to the B-vitamins and is a necessary nutrient, produced naturally by the body and related to lecithin (which is found in egg yolks). It's important because for years we've mistakenly been told to avoid eggs, and now egg consumption is down. Lecithin is an essential protector of every cell in our bodies and serves as the main source of choline. Because of this, it is essential in forming cell membranes and neurotransmitters, thus increasing energy and boosting memory. After eggs, other, less good sources are organ meats, dandelion greens, nuts, seeds, and soybeans. The recommended dose of choline is 1,500 mg. Take 500 mg three times a day with meals.

Alpha Lipoic Acid

This is a universal antioxidant that helps to protect both water- and fat-soluble vitamins and antioxidants. No other substance is capable of this. For the dieter, it encourages the body to convert food to energy more efficiently and helps to prevent what we eat from being deposited as fat. It's excellent for blood sugar regulation, helps to fight insulin resistance, and stimulates the cellular uptake of glucose. Therefore, it is very a important supplement for any overweight person. The recommended dose is 300 mg, taken in 100-mg doses three times a day with meals.

Weight-Loss Supplements That Are Not Recommended

Each of the following supplements is a stimulant, and they are often combined with each other to give a so-called boost to the metabolism. Although these products are somewhat well documented and have been proven to help people lose weight, it's always necessary to consider the long-term consequences of using something that artificially speeds up your metabolism. The Hamptons Diet is designed to *naturally* increase your rate of metabolism and teach you how to eat correctly for the rest of your life. Whenever you take something to speed up your metabolism, always be aware of what happens when you stop taking it: Your metabolism tends to slow down and that makes it harder for you to maintain your weight loss over an extended period of time.

Guarana is an herb that naturally contains caffeine, so you could easily ingest an overdose if you use it in combination with coffee, teas, or other beverages containing caffeine. The herbal form of ephedra contains five additional stimulants that are chemically related to methamphetamine and the decongestant synephrine. Other herbs of this type include ma huang and gotu kola. In the body, they constrict blood vessels, thus increasing blood pressure. They can also cause the release of stimulating neurotransmitters. Therefore, these herbs would not be good for anyone with hypertension or high blood pressure, anyone taking psychiatric medications such as Prozac or Paxil, or people who tend to be nervous and jittery. They can even cause excessive hair loss and an inability to sleep. I consider these herbs to be a throwback to the 1960s, when diet doctors prescribed amphetamines to their patients who wanted to lose weight—effective, but at what price? Ephedra has recently been banned by the FDA, but not other forms of guarana.

It is exciting that the science of nutrition is growing so quickly that I had to add one more item here as this book went to press. Although

I just mentioned that I do not recommend products that contain stimulants, I have to comment on a new supplement that is ideal for anyone trying to lose weight or maintain weight loss. The supplement is called Lean Mystique and is created by a company called Contemporary Nutrition. This is the first product of its kind that I have tested that did not cause me to have any jitters or nervous feelings; it left me with a complete sense of calmness and no feelings of hunger for at least eight or ten hours. I am always suspect of nutritional supplements that contain guarana, green tea extract, or any sort of caffeine. However, I am a perfect test case for products like this because I have not indulged in caffeine for at least twenty years. As a result, I am very sensitive to the slightest amount of caffeine. This supplement did what it said it would without any side effects that I noticed.

Lean Mystique works, in my opinion, because it contains twenty-two different ingredients—many new and all natural—that, when balanced together, help provide a sense of well-being and support optimal weight loss, which I encourage in this book. Most weight-loss management dietary supplements are based on only one ingredient or focused on one aspect of weight management, such as enhancing metabolism or curbing appetite. Lean Mystique, however, contains ingredients that minimize the jittery feeling, the mood swings that can be associated with carbohydrate restriction, the occasional gastric distress associated with changing to a healthier diet; it also helps maintain a normal glucose level and allows for a clear head and the mental energy to stay focused. The company even has a scientific advisory board; I was so impressed with this product that I may become part of the company. I think this supplement makes a perfect accompaniment to the Hamptons Diet. In the resource section of this book, I will provide details about how to get Lean Mystique.

Other things you may have heard about are liquid collagen–type products that one takes three hours before bedtime. The advertisements encourage people to eat whatever they normally eat—just not up to three hours before bedtime. I don't know the scientific reasoning behind these products (neither do the manufacturers, I'm sure), but not eating three hours before bedtime is probably not a bad idea and may be the reason for the weight loss. However, what I dislike most about these products is that they discourage a change in lifestyle, which is crucial for the overweight or obese person to learn.

For those of you unfamiliar with taking nutritional supplements, these suggestions can make it much easier to begin a protocol:

1. Start to take them gradually. Don't try to take the full recommended amount all at once. Divide them up throughout the day and build up to them, or you may risk getting an upset stomach. For example, if you want to take ten pills per day, start with three but split them up and take one with each meal. Then simply add another one each day, until you are up to the full amount. If you feel any stomach discomfort, decrease the amount you take and increase more slowly.

2. Buy decent brand-name supplements from manufacturers you can trust. If one brand is cheaper than the others, there's probably a reason for it. In the resources section, I mention some reputable companies.

3. Buy vitamins that have no artificial preservatives, artificial flavors, sweeteners, colorings, and yeast, dairy, egg, wheat, or soy by-products.

4. If you skip a dose of supplements, don't try to double up at the next meal—you will only waste them. If you miss a dose, consider that dose missed.

5. Most supplements need to be taken at least three times a day because they are not time released. So, don't think you can take a full day's amount at once and then forget about them for the rest of the day. Take only one dose at a time.

6. If you forget to take a supplement that should be taken on an empty stomach, then take it with the meal. It's better to take it that way than not at all.

7. Lay out all your supplements a few days or a week at a time, and then carry them around with you. Otherwise, organizing them will become too much of a chore.

CHAPTER 8

The Hamptons Diet Recipes

Ann became my patient about five years ago. She was overweight, had high blood pressure, and was beginning to develop diabetes. She was fifty-six years old and had watched her mother deteriorate in the same manner. She was determined not to let this happen to her. Ann was a very famous clothing designer with homes around the world and was friends with Hamptons and Hollywood royalty. She was often jetting around the world presenting her fashions at the collections. While this was very glamorous, it left her little time for exercising and too much time for socializing. Years ago, she kept her figure through the use of nicotine and illicit drugs, but now she needed someone to teach her how to eat, what to eat, and most importantly how to do so with a busy schedule. Although your schedule and mine may not be as glamorous as Ann's, fitting the proper foods into one's diet can be challenging for anyone. I put her on my *Thin For Good* diet plan, which I developed immediately after leaving the Atkins Center. She responded well and lost forty-one pounds. Her blood sugars returned to normal, but her blood pressure remained slightly elevated, as did her cholesterol level.

She stuck with the program and was thrilled to lose weight and get rid of her diabetes. She continued to see me for regular checkups. As soon as I learned of the benefits of monounsaturated-rich diets—and macadamia nut oil, in particular—I immediately switched her to this oil for all her cooking uses, even for salad dressings. I gave her a blood test before we began and then again three months and six months later.

After three months, her HDL cholesterol began to rise and her total cholesterol number had reduced from 275 to 237. We were both excited to see such improvement. At the end of six months, with no changes to her program except the addition of macadamia nut oil and an overall effort to keep her diet monounsaturated-rich, her HDL cholesterol had risen to 99 and her total cholesterol had dropped to 189. Her blood pressure finally returned to normal, and she was able to get rid of those blood pressure medications she so desperately feared. She also shed a few extra pounds, bringing her total weight loss to 48 pounds. She couldn't believe what a monounsaturated-rich approach could do for her or for anyone who was already on a lower-carbohydrate approach. "I can't believe what a difference the Australian macadamia nut oil made to my health," said Ann.

So, even if you follow a low-carbohydrate diet plan or have tried these diets in the past, the element that will make your diet really successful is being monounsaturated-rich. The Hamptons Diet provides you with the tools to be both thin and healthy.

The real beauty of monounsaturated-rich macadamia nut oil lies in the fact that it isn't overpowering. It can be used with delicate dishes such as fish, as a finishing oil, or is strong enough to hold its own as a frying oil. It's even great in many dishes that you wouldn't want to ruin with the assertive taste of olive oil, such as omelets, muffins, or pancakes. I learned how to use macadamia nut oil simply by substituting it in my old standard recipes. Wow! What a difference it made! If you don't like the following recipes, just switch the oil you use in everyday cooking with macadamia nut oil, to create a monounsaturated-rich diet. I promise, it will be as if you're eating entirely new foods—that's how much it enhances the flavor of any dish. In the meantime, enjoy the following recipes and send me some of your favorites, too.

It's really exciting to present these recipes to you. I prepared recipes for my previous books but was always a little uneasy because of the high heat required to cook some of the meals. I had to recommend olive oil because I knew of no other substitute that was both affordable and good for you. Now, I can give you recipes without any fear or hesitation because with Australian macadamia nut oil, you no longer have to be afraid of the trans-fatty acid formation that occurs when frying, sautéing, baking, or cooking with any other method that uses high heat. Even a light sauté reaches about 300 degrees F, and most oils start to decompose at that temperature.

Most of the following recipes use macadamia nut oil as their base. This ensures that you easily get the monounsaturated level that's necessary for good health. Now, if you don't like this oil or you run out of it, you can still follow the meal plans and recipes by using any oil you like. That's up to you. I'm simply relaying what has worked best with my patients on the Hamptons Diet and what has helped them in their quest to lose weight and become healthy. By using this type of oil, you'll get the perfect 1:1 balance of omega-6 to omega-3 fatty acids; the highest level of monounsaturated fats, about 85 percent; and a high smoke point, to boot. If you'd rather use another oil, please refer to the information located in chapter 5 and make the best decision, based on the information I've provided. My preferences other than Australian macadamia nut oil are

1. Estate-bottled extra virgin olive oil, preferably Australian
2. Avocado oil

Please, never use canola oil.

Every recipe is located somewhere in the meal plan section, so this diet will be easy for you to follow successfully. Given the ABCs of this program and the suggestions for making changes, the following recipes will provide enough variety for you to eat something different each day and night for many months to come. Also, in some recipes, I mention using a macadamia nut oil spray. This isn't available in stores, but many of you probably do this trick at home already. Simply fill a spray bottle made for oils with your Australian macadamia nut oil, and use that to coat grills, pans, and so on. The bottles can be found in many stores. They make cooking a lot easier, and you'll use less oil that way.

Breakfast Items

Atlantic Beach Avocado Boats

Yield: 4 servings　　　　　　　　　*Carbohydrates per serving: 8*

    2 ripe avocados, halved, pitted, and peeled
    1 tablespoon fresh-squeezed lime juice
    5 eggs, beaten
    4 olives, chopped
    2 green onions, minced fine
    ¼ cup fresh cilantro, chopped
    ¼ teaspoon fresh ground pepper
    2 tablespoons macadamia nut oil
    ½ teaspoon salt
    sour cream, if desired

Sprinkle avocado halves with lime juice and set aside. Mix eggs, olives, cilantro, and pepper in a medium bowl. Heat the oil in a large skillet. Add the egg mixture; cook, stirring occasionally to scramble the eggs, until they are cooked through, about 3 to 5 minutes. Sprinkle with salt to taste. Spoon the eggs into the avocado halves and serve. Dollop a spoonful of sour cream, if desired, to finish.

Asparagus with Mozzarella

Yield: 4 servings　　　　　　　　　*Carbohydrates per serving: 5*

    8 asparagus spears, boiled and chilled
    8 ounces fresh salted mozzarella
    handful fresh basil

This is a simple reminder that breakfast foods don't always have to be eggs. Simply boil some asparagus or use leftovers from the night before, then thinly slice some fresh salted mozzarella and arrange the slices between the asparagus. Season with fresh basil and a drizzle of macadamia nut oil.

Goat Cheese and Arugula Omelet

Yield: 2 servings   *Carbohydrates per serving: 4*

This will serve as your basic omelet recipe. You can substitute your favorite ingredients—as long as they're on your acceptable list—for the goat cheese and the arugula listed here.

4 eggs
2 tablespoons water
2 tablespoons heavy cream
salt
pepper
1 tablespoon grated parmesan cheese
1 tablespoon macadamia nut oil
2 large handfuls of arugula leaves, fresh from your garden
½ cup crumbled goat cheese

Whisk all the ingredients, except the goat cheese and the arugula, together in a bowl until frothy. Heat the oil in a skillet until hot. Sauté the arugula for 1 minute or until wilted. Pour the egg mixture over the greens and, as they begin to set, lift the edge of the eggs with a spatula to allow the liquid eggs to slide beneath the cooked eggs. Continue to cook over a low heat until the eggs are set but not too firm. Before they set too much, simply add the goat cheese or whatever other ingredient you choose. Fold the omelet in half and serve.

Wainscott Breakfast Torte

Yield: 8 servings *Carbohydrates per serving: 6*

For the pesto:

    1½ cups fresh basil leaves
    2 cloves garlic
    ¼ cup pine nuts
    ¾ cup macadamia nut oil

    6 large eggs
    1 teaspoon garlic powder
    1 teaspoon fresh chopped oregano
    1 teaspoon fresh chopped basil
    1 teaspoon fresh chopped thyme
    1 small onion, finely diced
    1 cup shredded parmesan cheese
    2 (6-ounce) cans of artichoke hearts, quartered

In a food processor, combine all the ingredients for the pesto except the oil, until the mixture forms a thick puree. When the mixture is thick, slowly add the oil until the pesto is the consistency of creamed butter. Set aside. Coat a 9- × 9-inch baking dish with macadamia nut oil spray. In a large mixing bowl, beat the eggs with the garlic powder and the fresh herbs. Add the pesto, and combine thoroughly. Reduce the speed to low, and add the onion and parmesan cheese. Stir in the drained artichoke hearts, and pour into the prepared dish. Level the top with a spatula, and bake in a preheated 400-degree F oven until lightly browned on the outside, about 45 minutes.

Baked Eggs with 2 Cheeses

Yield: 2 servings   *Carbohydrates per serving: 4*

1 tablespoon macadamia nut oil
1 tablespoon minced green onion
2 teaspoons fresh chopped herbs (basil, oregano, or whatever is fresh that day)
4 large eggs
1 ounce parmesan cheese, freshly grated
white pepper
salt

Pour ½ tablespoon of the oil into each of two ramekins. Divide the onion and herbs between the two dishes. Break two eggs into each ramekin over the herbs and onion and sprinkle evenly with the parmesan. Bake in a preheated 400-degree F oven for 8 to 10 minutes. Season with salt and pepper, and serve.

Cabo Pork Posole

Yield: 12 servings   *Carbohydrates per serving: 6*

2 tablespoons macadamia nut oil
1 small onion, chopped
1 green bell pepper, chopped
two 32-ounce containers chicken broth—low sodium
one 14½-ounce can tomatillos
1 pound shredded pork—preferably left over from a previous meal
1 teaspoon pepper
½ teaspoon salt
½ teaspoon ground cumin
2 tablespoons chopped fresh cilantro
2 tablespoons fresh lime juice
sour cream for garnish

Pour the oil into a large heavy saucepan. Sauté the onion and green pepper in the hot oil over medium-high heat for 5 minutes. Stir in the chicken broth and the next five ingredients, and bring to a boil. Reduce the heat and simmer, stirring occasionally, for 20 minutes. Remove from the heat, and stir in the cilantro and lime juice. Pour into bowls, and garnish with a dollop of sour cream.

Quiche Florentine

Yield: 6 servings   *Carbohydrates per serving: 6*

2 tablespoons macadamia nut oil + macadamia nut oil spray
1 (8-ounce) package fresh mushrooms, chopped
1 roasted red bell pepper, chopped
1 cup heavy whipping cream
3 large eggs
½ teaspoon fresh chopped basil
½ teaspoon fresh chopped parsley
½ teaspoon oregano
½ teaspoon black pepper
½ teaspoon salt
⅛ teaspoon ground red pepper
1 cup chopped fresh spinach
6 ounces of swiss cheese, shredded

Heat the oil in a large skillet over medium-high heat. Add the mush-rooms and bell pepper, and sauté for 8 minutes or until tender. Whisk together the cream and the next seven ingredients in a large bowl. Stir in the mushroom mixture, spinach, and cheese. Pour into a nonstick 9-inch pie pan that has been sprayed with macadamia nut oil. Place on the lowest rack of a preheated 400-degree F oven for 40 minutes or until set. Let stand for 10 minutes, then remove from the pan onto a serving dish. Alternatively, if you really want to get fancy, place the mixture into an oiled springform pan and place that in an inch of water inside another pan to form a bain-marie. Cook for 60 minutes at 375 degrees F. Remove from oven and take out of the bath. Allow to cool for 10 minutes before plating and serving.

Conscience Point Quiche

Yield: 6 servings   *Carbohydrates per serving: 6*

    2 tablespoons macadamia nut oil + macadamia nut oil spray
    4 green onions, chopped into a fine dice
    12 ounces of fresh crabmeat
    1 teaspoon grated lemon rind
    ½ teaspoon Old Bay Seasoning
    ⅛ teaspoon ground red pepper
    1 cup heavy whipping cream
    3 large eggs
    ½ teaspoon black pepper
    ½ teaspoon salt
    6 ounces of parmesan cheese, shredded

This is a variation on the previous recipe and is made the exact same way, except: In the large skillet, place the first 5 ingredients in the heated oil and sauté for 2 to 3 minutes. Then follow the previous recipe exactly.

Ricotta Pignoli Muffins

Yield: 6 servings   *Carbohydrates per serving: 4*

    1 cup ricotta
    2 large eggs
    ½ cup parmesan cheese
    ½ teaspoon salt
    2 packets of Stevia
    ½ teaspoon vanilla extract
    1 ounce pignoli nuts, toasted and crushed

In a medium bowl, combine the ricotta and eggs, and mix until smooth. Add the parmesan, salt, Stevia, and vanilla, and mix again until smooth. Mix the nuts throughout the batter. Pour into a nonstick muffin pan. If you don't have a nonstick pan, spray your muffin pan with macadamia nut oil or line the muffin tin with muffin soufflé paper. Pour an equal amount of batter into each muffin indentation, and place in a preheated 350-degree F oven for 15 to 20 minutes.

Variation

Ricotta Macadamia Nut Muffins: Switch the nut you add to 2 ounces macadamia nuts, and follow the previous recipe exactly, for another breakfast treat.

Frittata with Queso Blanco and Peppers

Yield: 4 servings   *Carbohydrates per serving: 3*

Again, this recipe can be used as a basis for as many variations as you can think of.

    3 tablespoons macadamia nut oil
    ½ Spanish onion, diced
    1 bell pepper, seeded and diced
    2 scallions, chopped
    ¼ pound button mushrooms, sliced
    5 eggs
    salt
    pepper to taste
    2 ounces manchego cheese, cubed

In a sauté pan, heat oil over medium flame for 30 seconds. Add the first four ingredients, and sauté for 3 to 4 minutes over medium heat or until tender. Meanwhile, whip the eggs, salt, and pepper in a bowl with a whisk. Pour the egg mixture into the sauté pan, and distribute the cheese evenly. Remove from flame, and place in the oven for 15 to 18 minutes, or until a jiggle of the pan reveals a loose center. Remove, and run a rubber spatula around the perimeter of the pan to loosen the eggs, then slide onto a serving dish. Allow to cool slightly, and serve.

Variations

Zucchini and Mushroom: Simply dice up 1 small yellow squash and ¼ cup cremini mushrooms.

Greens: Simply add spinach and arugula.

Corned Beef Hash

Yield: 4 servings   *Carbohydrates per serving: 5*

1 (3-pound) corned beef
1 cup cabbage, shredded
1 dill pickle
salt
pepper
2 tablespoons macadamia nut oil
4 ounces cheddar cheese, grated

Place the corned beef in a large stockpot, and cover with water. Bring to a boil, reduce the heat to simmer, cover, and cook for 3 hours. Add the shredded cabbage to the water, and simmer for another 30 minutes. Remove the beef from the pot, and allow to rest until it can be handled. Remove any excess fat or gristle. Drain the cabbage, and set aside. Puree the dill pickle in a blender or a food processor. Cube half the corned beef and shred the other half. In a large bowl, mix the corned beef, pickle, and cabbage. Season to taste. In a large skillet, heat the oil until warm over medium-high heat. Add the corned beef mixture, and press down with a spatula. Cook until crisp, turning once. Divide the hash among four plates, sprinkle the cheese over each dish, and serve.

Laredo Baked Eggs

Yield: 4 servings   *Carbohydrates per serving: 4*

1½ cups heavy cream
4 tablespoons parmesan cheese, freshly grated
macadamia nut oil spray
¼ pound hot pork sausage, crumbled
1 tablespoon macadamia nut oil
1 green onion, very thinly sliced
1 green pepper, roasted and peeled, cut into thin strips
1 jalapeno, seeded and finely minced
1 clove garlic, finely minced
kosher salt
10 eggs
8 ounces shredded Monterey Jack cheese
freshly ground black pepper

Combine cream and parmesan in a medium bowl, and whisk until frothy. In a large skillet, spray a little oil and add the sausage, cooking over high heat until browned, about 4 minutes. Set on paper towels, and drain excess fat from the skillet. Add the tablespoon of oil and heat. When hot, add the onion, roasted green pepper, jalapeno, garlic, and salt. Cook over medium-high heat until the onions are translucent, about 5 minutes. Remove from heat, and add the sausage, eggs, 1⅓ cup cheese, and black pepper, and mix well. Spray a 10-inch baking dish with the oil to lightly cover. Sprinkle ⅓ cup cheese onto the bottom of the baking dish. Pour in the egg mixture, being careful to distribute the ingredients evenly. Sprinkle the remaining cheese on top, and bake in a preheated 350-degree F oven for about 60 minutes or until a toothpick inserted in the center comes out clean.

To Grill a Pepper—Cut into strips, remove the seeds, arrange on a foil-lined baking sheet, and broil until blackened, about 8 minutes. Remove from heat, wrap the foil around the pepper, and allow to steam. When cool enough to handle, remove the skins. This method can be used to roast any type of pepper. The timing may be a little more or a little less, depending on the variety.

Soy Macadamia Nut Pancakes

Yield: 4 servings   *Carbohydrates per serving of 4 pancakes: 6*

This can be made in two ways. The first is from scratch, as I'll illustrate here. The second is by using one of the many low-carb pancake mixes that are currently available. The one that I currently think tastes the best is Low Carb Success, which can be found in many low-carb sections of your local supermarket or health food store. Or, you can contact the manufacturer directly at http://www.lowcarbsuccess.org. When following the recipe, make sure you use macadamia nut oil as the oil. It tastes much better that way. Otherwise, this is how you would make it from scratch:

½ cup soy flour or soy protein isolate

3 eggs

¼ cup water

¼ cup heavy cream

2 ounces crushed macadamia nuts

¼ teaspoon salt

macadamia nut oil

Combine the first six ingredients in a mixing bowl, and mix thoroughly with a whisk. Note that there should be lumps. Spray a large skillet or griddle with a light coating of oil. When the oil is hot, pour about 1 tablespoon of the batter onto the griddle or skillet, cooking evenly on both sides, about 1 minute for each. Continue until all the batter is used.

Variation

Any nut can be used in this recipe; for example, you can make Soy Pecan Pancakes, too.

Fresh Strawberry Topping

Yield: 1 serving   *Carbohydrates per serving: 2*

This can be done with any of your favorite berries to add variety to your breakfast.

    5 fresh berries, diced

Put the diced berries in a blender or a food processor and process until smooth. Pour over the pancakes to use as a syrup.

Farmers' Market Salad

Yield: 8 servings   *Carbohydrates per serving: 6*

    16 ounces of mixed organic greens
    2 large avocados, chopped
    1 large cucumber, peeled and sliced
    ½ cup sliced almonds, toasted
    4 ounces crumbled feta cheese
    ½ teaspoon fresh chopped basil
    salt to taste
    pepper to taste

Combine all the ingredients in a large bowl, and sprinkle with salt and pepper to taste. Dress with your favorite low-carbohydrate salad dressing. Please see the salad dressings section of this book for some options.

Big Benedict with Chipotle Hollandaise

Yield: 8 servings   *Carbohydrates per serving, including sauce: 5*

Chipotle Hollandaise Sauce (see next recipe)
8 large eggs, poached
1 cup shredded Monterey Jack cheese with peppers
1 cup salsa—your favorite salsa will do here, as long as it doesn't contain sugar
8 teaspoons sour cream

Ladle a small portion of the hollandaise sauce onto each plate. Then put the poached egg onto the center of the plate, place some shredded cheeses and salsa on top of each egg, drizzle more of the hollandaise sauce on each egg, and top with a dollop of sour cream.

Chipotle Hollandaise Sauce

Yield: 1½ cups   *Carbohydrates per serving: 5*

4 large egg yolks
2 tablespoons fresh lemon juice
1 cup butter, melted
1 tablespoon fresh minced cilantro
4 teaspoons pureed chipotle peppers in adobo sauce. This ingredient can be found in the international section of your supermarket or in Latin grocery stores in a can.
¼ teaspoon salt

Whisk the yolks in the top of a double boiler, then gradually whisk in the lemon juice. Place over hot water that's in the bottom of the double boiler (do not boil). Add butter, ⅓ cup at a time, whisking until smooth; whisk in the cilantro; whisk until smooth; whisk in the peppers and then the salt. Cook, whisking constantly, about 10 minutes or until thickened and a thermometer registers 160 degrees F. Serve immediately.

Strawberry Breakfast Smoothie

Yield: 1 serving   *Carbohydrates per serving: 6*

    2 ripe strawberries, cut into small pieces
    2 ounces heavy whipping cream
    8 ounces water
    1 scoop soy or whey protein powder (unsweetened)
    ice
    1 tablespoon macadamia nut oil

Combine all ingredients in a blender and liquefy. I add the macadamia nut oil to this recipe because a tablespoon a day may keep the doctor away. This is how heart patients in Australia use it to lower cholesterol and stay healthy. You can choose not to add this, but it makes the drink extra rich and smooth.

Variation

You can add 1 tablespoon of peanut butter to make this a little thicker, which would increase the carbohydrate count per serving by 2.

Meier's Path Scrambled Eggs

Yield: 4 servings   *Carbohydrates per serving: 2*

    1 pound Mexican chorizo, removed from casing and crumbled
    3 tablespoons macadamia nut oil
    1 small onion, finely chopped
    1 small serrano chili, finely chopped
    6 eggs
    2 ounces heavy cream
    1 teaspoon grated parmesan cheese
    kosher salt
    1 cup shredded Monterey Jack cheese

In a 10-inch skillet, combine the chorizo, oil, onion, and chili. Cook over medium-high heat for 4 to 5 minutes, until the sausage is cooked and the onion is translucent. Remove from heat, and drain the liquid. In a stainless steel bowl, beat the eggs with the heavy cream, pinch of salt, and parmesan cheese. Add the eggs to the cooked chorizo mixture in the skillet. Scramble the eggs over medium heat until firm, about 2 minutes. Remove to plates and sprinkle the Monterey Jack over each serving.

Asparagus with Buffalo Mozzarella

Yield: 2 servings   *Carbohydrates per serving: 4*

    8 stalks asparagus, peeled and trimmed
    macadamia nut oil and vinegar dressing
    4 ounces fresh buffalo mozzarella
    1 marinated red pepper, sliced into thin strips
    freshly grated black pepper

Boil the asparagus in salted water for 5 minutes or until crisp-tender;
drain and immediately submerge in an ice bath; drain. Place the
asparagus in a shallow dish, pour some oil and vinegar dressing over
it, and refrigerate. This can be made the night before, so that your
breakfast is waiting for you when you wake up. When you're ready,
plate the asparagus, slice the mozzarella into two even pieces, and
place on the bottom of the stalks. Gently lay the red pepper over the
asparagus. Dust the plate with black pepper, and serve.

Scrambled Eggs with Sautéed Vegetables

Yield: 2 servings   *Carbohydrates per serving: This will depend
on which vegetables you add or how
much cheese. As stated, it is 4.*

This will serve as your basic scrambled egg recipe. There are as many
variations on this as your imagination can dream up using the items
on your food lists. Have fun with this one, and remember to change it
often so that you don't get bored.

    2 tablespoons macadamia nut oil (you may not need the oil if you're
        using a meat such as sausage or bacon, as the meat will produce
        its own oil while cooking, so only use the oil if you're adding a
        vegetable base to your scrambled eggs)
    2 asparagus spears, peeled and finely chopped
    ½ red pepper, seeded and finely chopped
    ½ yellow pepper, seeded and finely chopped

½ small white onion, finely diced
4 eggs
1 ounce water
2 ounces heavy cream
1 ounce grated parmesan cheese
salt
pepper

Heat the oil in a skillet over medium-high heat. When heated, sauté the chopped vegetables for about 5 minutes or just until soft. Whisk the eggs, water, heavy cream, and parmesan cheese in a bowl until well mixed. Then add the egg mixture to the skillet (if using meat in this recipe, you may want to drain the excess grease out of the pan before adding the eggs). Scramble the eggs, season with salt and pepper, and cook until firm, about 2 minutes.

Lunch Items

North of the Highway Hot Dogs

Yield: 4 servings   *Carbohydrates per serving: 2*

4 hot dogs, preferably without preservatives
¼ cup Maconnaise (see recipe on page 205)
¼ cup mustard
4 lettuce leaves
4 onion slices

Cut a slit lengthwise through each hot dog, cutting to, but not through, the other side. Place hot dogs flat side down in a skillet, and cook until browned, about 2 minutes on each side. Drain hot dogs on a paper towel. Stir together the Maconnaise and mustard. Lay out the lettuce leaves, and place one hot dog in each leaf. Spoon the mayo mixture onto each hot dog, and garnish with the onion slices.

Town Line Eggs

Yield: 4 servings   *Carbohydrates per serving: 6*
                                            (including the pico de gallo)

1 cup of pico de gallo (see next recipe), chopped fine
12 hard-cooked eggs, cut in half
½ cup sour cream
hot sauce, to taste
sea salt
fresh ground black pepper
1½ cups guacamole
2 tablespoons fresh red pepper, finely diced
2 tablespoons fresh yellow pepper, finely diced
fresh chopped cilantro leaves for garnish

Drain the pico de gallo for about 1 hour in the refrigerator so that you are left with a dry product. Chop the yolks from 6 of the eggs, and add to the pico; stir this by hand in a small stainless steel mixing bowl. Fold the sour cream into this mixture, and season to taste with the hot sauce, salt, and pepper. Spoon or pipe this into 12 egg halves. Take the remaining 6 yolks, chop them, and combine with the guacamole. For the Guacamole recipe, please see the Sag Taco recipe in this section. Add red and yellow peppers, and season to taste with more salt and pepper. Spoon into the remaining 12 egg halves. Divide onto 4 plates, and garnish with an additional dollop of sour cream and some fresh chopped cilantro leaves.

Pico de Gallo

Yield: 16 servings   *Carbohydrates per serving: 2*

I prefer mine spicy, so I use ancho chilies. You don't have to use chilies at all. For a milder pico, simply eliminate this ingredient. This recipe can be used for any of the dishes that call for pico de gallo.

8 ancho chilies, seeded and deveined
2 ripe farm-stand tomatoes, seeded and chopped fine
1 medium onion, chopped fine
4 cloves garlic, finely diced
¾ cup macadamia nut oil
¼ cup red wine vinegar
¼ cup green bell pepper
1 teaspoon chopped fresh oregano
large bunch of cilantro, chopped fine
½ cup fresh-squeezed lime juice

Roast the ancho chilies in an iron skillet over medium-high heat for 5 minutes. During this time, the skin will blister. Chop into ¼-inch pieces. Soak briefly in hot water to cover in a small bowl, then drain. Combine the anchos, tomatoes, onion, garlic, oil, and vinegar in a medium stainless steel bowl. Mix well, and let marinate at room temperature for 2 hours. Put in a food processor and pulse until all the ingredients are chopped fine. Then add in, one at a time, the pepper, oregano, cilantro, and lime juice until well combined.

Turkey and Swiss Roll-Ups

Carbohydrates per Roll-up: 1

This is an easy-to-prepare recipe to take to lunch or send with the kids to school or camp. You simply take a slice of deli turkey, spread mustard on it, then lay a slice of swiss cheese over the mustard, and roll them up. If you're taking these on the road, skewer them with toothpicks to hold them together. You can even add lettuce leaves to the roll-up if you want a little crunch. Any deli meat and cheese will work for this recipe.

East Asian Chicken Soup

Yield: 6 servings   *Carbohydrates per serving: 3*

   6 cups fat-free, low-sodium chicken broth
   1 large egg, slightly beaten
   1 tablespoon soy sauce (lite, without sugar)
   2 green onions, green parts only, chopped
   6 ounces shiitake mushrooms, chopped
   2 cups fresh spinach
   1½ pounds cooked chicken breast, removed from bone

In a large, heavy saucepan, bring the broth to a boil; reduce heat immediately, and allow to simmer. Slowly add the egg, stirring constantly until the egg forms lacy strands. Immediately remove from heat. Let stand for 1 minute. Stir in the soy sauce, green onions, and shiitake mushrooms. Place the spinach and chicken in bowls; ladle the soup over the chicken and the spinach. Serve immediately.

Artichoke and Shrimp Chowder

Yield: 8 servings   *Carbohydrates per serving: 8*

   3 tablespoons macadamia nut oil
   1 small onion, finely chopped
   2 garlic cloves, minced
   3 ribs celery, peeled and cut along the diagonal into a small dice
   1 (6-ounce) can artichoke hearts
   24 ounces reduced-sodium chicken broth, organic
   1 teaspoon dried thyme
   1 bay leaf
   1 teaspoon red pepper
   4 ounces heavy cream
   kosher salt
   pepper
   2 tablespoons cauliflower puree
   1 pound small uncooked shrimp
   ½ cup chopped cilantro for garnish

In a large stockpot, heat the oil and add the onion, garlic, celery, and artichoke hearts, then sauté for about 5 minutes until the onion is translucent. Gradually stir in the broth, and bring to a simmer. Add all the other ingredients except the shrimp and cilantro leaves, and simmer for 1 hour, allowing it to reduce. Add 1 tablespoon of cauliflower puree to thicken, and allow to simmer for another half hour. If not yet at desired thickness, add another tablespoon of cauliflower puree or continue to simmer for another 30 minutes. Finally, add the shrimp, cook for 10 minutes, and serve garnished with cilantro leaves.

Sag Taco Salad

Yield: 6 servings   *Carbohydrates per serving: 5*

4 tablespoons macadamia nut oil
1 pound ground beef
1 small onion, chopped
1 garlic clove, minced
1 tablespoon fajita seasoning mix
1 (12-ounce) jar salsa verde
½ head iceberg lettuce, shredded
Guacamole (see next recipe)
sour cream, if desired

In a large skillet, heat half the oil over medium-high heat. Add the beef, stirring until the beef crumbles and is no longer pink, about 8 minutes. Drain, pat dry with paper towels, and set aside. In the same skillet, heat the remaining half of the oil, add the onion and garlic, and sauté for 1 minute. Return the beef to the skillet; add the fajita seasonings and half the salsa verde. Cook over medium-high heat 3 minutes or until thoroughly heated and the liquid has evaporated. Divide the shredded iceberg lettuce among 6 plates, pour the beef mixture onto the lettuce; divide the Guacamole among the plates, laying it on top of the beef mixture, then garnish with the remaining salsa verde, and a dollop of sour cream, if desired.

Guacamole

Yield: 1½ cups   *Carbohydrates per serving: 5*

    2 avocados
    2 scallions, chopped very fine
    1 small onion, chopped very fine
    ½ teaspoon salt
    ½ teaspoon fresh chopped coriander
    ½ teaspoon chili powder
    1 tablespoon lime juice

In a small bowl, mash the avocados until smooth, add the remaining
ingredients, and mix together well.

Mushroom-Filled Goat Cheese Burger

Yield: 4 servings   *Carbohydrates per serving: 3*

    1 pound ground chuck (85% lean)—anything leaner
        will cause drier burgers
    kosher salt
    freshly ground black pepper
    3 tablespoons minced scallion, white part only
    1 tablespoon grated fresh ginger
    1 cup crumbled blue cheese
    2 tablespoons macadamia nut oil
    ½ cup chopped onion
    1 garlic clove, minced
    ¾ pound chopped white mushrooms
    spinach leaves (raw)

In a stainless steel bowl, combine the first five ingredients (up to the
cheese), until mixed well. Form this mixture into 8 hamburger patties.
Press an equal amount of cheese on 4 of the patties, and refrigerate. In
the meantime, heat the oil in a small skillet, add the onion and garlic,
and sauté for 5 minutes. Then add the mushrooms, and cook for about
7 minutes or until the mushrooms release their juices. Drain, remove

the burgers from the refrigerator, evenly divide the mushroom/ onion/garlic mixture among the four burgers, then cover with the other 4. Seal the edges with your fingers, and refrigerate again. On a preheated medium-high grill, sear each side for 3 to 4 minutes for medium or until they reach desired doneness. Serve on a bed of spinach leaves.

Long Beach Shrimp Salad

Yield: 6 servings   *Carbohydrates per serving: 4*

    2 tablespoons mustard seeds
    2 tablespoons macadamia nut oil
    ½ red bell pepper, seeded, de-ribbed, and diced
    ½ cup chopped fresh parsley
    2 tablespoons Dijon mustard
    ¼ cup Maconnaise (see recipe on page 205)
    ½ cup sour cream
    1 tablespoon fresh lime juice
    1 teaspoon fresh tarragon, minced
    1 pound small shrimp, boiled
    sea salt
    freshly ground white pepper
    5 heads Belgian endive

In a small skillet, heat the mustard seeds over medium heat until they pop. Let them cool, and then mix with the pepper, parsley, mustard, Maconnaise, sour cream, lime juice, and tarragon until well combined. Add the shrimp, and mix gently. Season with salt and pepper to taste. Separate the leaves of the endive, and select 36 of the best leaves. Put 1 tablespoon of the mixture onto each leaf, and arrange on a plate. Each plate gets 6 filled leaves. Sprinkle each plate with additional tarragon, and serve.

Cold Devon Asparagus Soup with Lemon Crème Fraiche

Yield: 6 servings   *Carbohydrates per serving: 6*

1½ pounds asparagus, trimmed and peeled
2 leeks, white and light green parts only, thinly sliced
4 tablespoons macadamia nut oil
2 tablespoons white wine vinegar
salt
freshly ground coarse black pepper
3½ cups of vegetable or chicken broth
crème fraiche for garnish
3 chives, chopped finely for garnish

Place the asparagus and leeks in a large roasting pan. Add the oil, vinegar, salt, and pepper to taste. Mix so that the vegetables are well coated. Roast in a preheated 425-degree F oven, stirring occasionally, until the asparagus is tender, about 15 minutes. Let cool, and transfer to a food processor. Puree in batches with the broth until the soup is smooth. Strain through a fine sieve or a cheesecloth. Chill thoroughly and then garnish with a dollop of crème fraiche and chives.

Lemon Crème Fraiche

½ cup crème fraiche
1 teaspoon fresh lemon zest

In a small stainless steel bowl, whisk together the crème fraiche and the fresh lemon zest.

Roast Beef Rolls with Mustard Horseradish Crème à la Brent's

Yield: 6 servings   *Carbohydrates per serving: 7*

2 tablespoons macadamia nut oil
1 medium onion, halved and sliced
1 yellow bell pepper, halved and sliced
6 romaine lettuce leaves
Mustard-Horseradish Crème (see next recipe)
1 pound roast beef, thinly sliced

In a large skillet, heat the oil and sauté the onion and bell pepper over medium heat for 2 minutes or until just tender. Lay out the large lettuce leaves, one per plate. Spread the Mustard-Horseradish Crème onto each leaf. Next, lay the roast beef into each leaf. Divide the bell pepper and onion mixture evenly into each leaf and onto the roast beef, then finish with the remaining mustard mixture.

Mustard-Horseradish Crème

Yield: 1 cup

  1 cup sour cream or crème fraiche
  3 tablespoons horseradish
  1 teaspoon dry mustard
  ¼ teaspoon lemon rind

Stir together all ingredients in a small bowl. Chill until ready to serve.

Sayre's Path Broccoli Casserole

Yield: 6 servings   *Carbohydrates per serving: 7*

  macadamia nut oil spray
  1 head fresh broccoli, chopped fine
  1 (10-ounce) can cream of mushroom soup
  2 cups diced cooked ham
  2 cups shredded cheddar cheese
  8 ounces sour cream
  white pepper
  ½ teaspoon dried mustard
  2 ounce parmesan cheese, freshly grated

Spray a casserole dish with macadamia nut oil. In a large mixing bowl, combine all the ingredients except the parmesan cheese, and mix well. Season to taste. Pour into the casserole dish, and cook uncovered for 30 minutes in a preheated 400-degree F oven. Increase temperature to 450 degrees. Then pour the parmesan cheese over the casserole, and cook for another 5 minutes or until brown and bubbly on top.

Egg Salad Maconnaise

Yield: 2 servings   *Carbohydrates per serving: 2*

This is simply your egg salad recipe or mine, but instead of using regular mayonnaise, you use Maconnaise.

    4 hard-boiled eggs, finely chopped
    1 tablespoon Maconnaise (see recipe on page 205)
    salt
    pepper
    1 teaspoon horseradish
    ½ teaspoon crushed red pepper
    ¼ onion, shredded
    1 stalk celery, finely diced
    1 teaspoon Dijon mustard

Combine all the ingredients in a stainless steel bowl until well mixed. Season to taste.

Variations

Instead of eggs, use tuna, either canned for the kids or fresh for you; salmon, canned or fresh, preferably wild; or boiled chicken breasts (also, leftover grilled chicken breast from a barbecue the night before works well in this recipe).

Stuffed Burgers à la Halsey

Yield: 4 servings   *Carbohydrates per serving: 2*

    1 pound ground chuck (85% lean)—anything leaner will cause drier
        burgers
    kosher salt
    freshly ground black pepper
    small green onion, white part only, finely diced
    2 tablespoons Italian parsley, finely minced
    1 teaspoon rice vinegar
    1 cup crumbled blue cheese
    raw spinach leaves

In a stainless steel bowl, combine all the ingredients, except the cheese, until mixed well. Form this mixture into 8 hamburger patties.

Press an equal amount of cheese on 4 of the patties, and cover with the other 4. Seal the edges with your fingers, and refrigerate. On a preheated medium-high grill, sear each side for 3 to 4 minutes for medium or until it reaches desired doneness. Serve on a bed of spinach leaves.

Peconica Dogs

Yield: 8 servings   *Carbohydrates per serving: 4*

    8 hot dogs, preferably organic and without preservatives
    4 ounces cheddar cheese, shredded
    ½ cup favorite salsa
    1 cup iceberg lettuce, shredded
    sour cream, if desired
    Guacamole, if desired

Cook hot dogs in boiling water for 5 minutes. Combine the cheese and the salsa in a glass bowl, and microwave on high for 1 minute or until thoroughly heated, stirring once. Cut a small slit on one side of the hot dog so that it lies flat on the plate. Spread the heated mixture on top of the hot dogs, and top evenly with shredded lettuce, sour cream, and Guacamole, if desired.

Settler's Asparagus

Yield: 4 servings   *Carbohydrates per serving: 5*

    2 pounds asparagus, peeled and trimmed
    6 tablespoons butter
    2 tablespoons macadamia nut oil
    4 eggs
    sea salt
    fresh ground white pepper
    8 thin slices of prosciutto
    parmigiano-reggiano cheese for slicing, about ½ pound

Steam the asparagus until it is crisp-tender, about 3 to 4 minutes. Immediately remove from water, place in an ice bath to stop the cooking process, and drain. Melt the butter in a small saucepan over low heat. In a large skillet, heat the oil over medium-high heat, and crack the eggs into the skillet. Cook through, stirring in the salt and pepper until the whites are no longer runny, about 5 minutes. Divide the asparagus among four plates, and top with the prosciutto, butter, and a few slices of the cheese.

Acabonac Cheesecake

Yield: 12 servings   *Carbohydrates per serving: 6*

½ cup minced dried tomatoes in oil
2 (8-ounce) packages cream cheese, softened
3 large eggs
6 ounces swiss cheese, shredded
3 green onions, chopped
½ teaspoon salt
½ teaspoon pepper
¼ teaspoon ground red pepper
macadamia nut oil spray
1¾ cups sour cream

Drain the tomatoes well, pressing them between paper towels, and set aside. Beat cream cheese at medium speed with an electric mixer 2 to 3 minutes or until light and fluffy. Add eggs, one at a time, beating well after each addition. Stir in the tomatoes, swiss cheese, onions, salt, pepper, and red pepper, mixing well. Pour into a springform pan lined with waxed paper that has been sprayed with the oil. Bake on the lower rack in a preheated oven at 350 degrees F for 35 to 40 minutes or until a toothpick inserted in the center comes out clean. Remove from the oven, and spread the sour cream evenly over the top. Cool on a wire rack for 20 minutes, cover, and refrigerate for 8 hours. Place cheesecake on serving plate; release and remove the sides of the pan, remove the waxed paper, and serve.

Bacon Lettuce Turkey Twist

Yield: 6 servings   *Carbohydrates per serving: 2*

½ pound fresh mozzarella, cut into ½-inch pieces
1 cup macadamia nut oil and red wine vinegar dressing
½ cup kalamata olives, pitted and halved
2 green onions, sliced
2 tablespoons chopped fresh basil
1 tablespoon chopped fresh thyme
¼ teaspoon pepper
6 large outer romaine lettuce leaves
1 pound thinly sliced fresh turkey breast
10 bacon slices, cooked and crumbled
3 cups chopped romaine lettuce

Combine the mozzarella and the dressing in a shallow dish or a reseal-able plastic bag; cover or seal, and chill for 1 hour. Toss together the olives, the next four ingredients, and the mozzarella mixture. Let stand for 20 minutes. Lay out the large lettuce leaves on each plate, and divide the turkey evenly among the leaves. Then divide the mixture among the turkey/lettuce boats, and sprinkle each one with bacon and the chopped romaine leaves.

Southwestern BLT

This recipe is the same as the previous one, except that you substitute 1 teaspoon of chipotle powder and 1 teaspoon of Tabasco sauce for the basil and thyme. The preparation and the carbohydrate count per serving are identical.

Chihuahua Chicken Salad

Yield: 6 servings   *Carbohydrates per serving: 6*

    macadamia nut oil spray
    4 roasted red bell peppers
    2 cups chopped cooked chicken
    1 (8-ounce) package cream cheese, softened
    ¼ cup chopped ripe olives
    ½ small onion, finely diced
    4 ounces chopped green chilies
    2 tablespoons chopped fresh cilantro
    ½ teaspoon pepper
    ¼ cup pine nuts, toasted
    large iceberg lettuce leaves

To roast peppers, simply spray a generous coating of macadamia nut oil on them. Preheat the oven to broil. When the oven is hot, place the peppers under the broiler for 1 to 2 minutes per side. It doesn't matter if they burn on the outside. Remove from heat, and peel off the outer layer. An alternate way to do this, for people who are afraid of the broiler, is to place the peppers in a 350-degree F oven for 15 minutes, turning them once.

Chop the roasted peppers. In a large bowl, mix together the peppers, the chicken, and the next 6 ingredients. Cover and chill for 2 hours. Stir the pine nuts into the mixture, spoon evenly into the lettuce leaves, and close with toothpicks, if desired.

Backyard Steak Salad

Yield: 8 servings   *Carbohydrates per serving: 3*

This recipe takes some advance preparation time.

    4 (8-ounce) rib-eye steaks
    salt to taste
    pepper to taste
    1 teaspoon fresh chopped thyme
    1 teaspoon fresh chopped basil
    2 teaspoons ground cumin
    macadamia nut oil spray
    3 romaine lettuce hearts
    Salad Dressing (recipe follows)
    1 medium red onion, sliced into very thin rings

Season the steaks with salt and pepper. Place the thyme, basil, and cumin in a small dish. Spray the steaks with a light coating of macadamia nut oil, and rub them in the spice mixture. Allow to season for at least 2 hours or up to 24 hours, if preferred.

Preheat the grill. Grill the steaks to desired doneness, about 8 minutes on each side for medium, and keep them warm. Divide the romaine leaves onto eight plates. Dress the salads individually, then slice the steaks thinly and arrange on the salad.

Before serving, put two slices of red onion on top of each steak, add another dollop of dressing, and salad.

Salad Dressing

    ½ cup Maconnaise (see recipe on page 205)
    1 green onion, white part only, minced
    1 clove garlic, minced
    2 tablespoons fresh Italian parsley, minced
    1 cup heavy whipping cream
    2 teaspoons lime juice
    2 teaspoons white wine vinegar
    8 ounces artisanal blue cheese, crumbled
    salt and pepper to taste

Prepare the dressing by mixing all the ingredients in a small bowl until well blended. It can be made up to 48 hours in advance.

Quogue Kebabs

Yield: 4 servings   *Carbohydrates per serving: 6*

    4 skinned and boned chicken breast halves
    ½ cup macadamia nut oil
    2 tablespoons lite soy sauce
    1 teaspoon ground ginger
    1 teaspoon garlic powder
    8 (8-inch) wooden or metal skewers
    8 small green onions
    8 large mushrooms
    1 green bell pepper, cut into 1-inch pieces

Cut the chicken into 2 × 1-inch strips. Whisk together the oil and the next three ingredients, reserving ¼ cup oil for basting. Pour the remaining marinade into a shallow dish, and add the chicken strips. Cover and chill for at least 2 hours, turning the chicken occasionally. Soak the wooden skewers, if that is your preference, in water for 30 minutes to prevent burning. Remove the chicken from the marinade and discard the liquid. Spear the chicken and the vegetables onto the eight skewers. Grill the chicken on a preheated grill, over medium-high heat, covered—about 15 or 20 minutes, turning occasionally and basting with the reserved marinade.

South Hampton Scallops Provençal

Yield: 4 servings   *Carbohydrates per serving: 4*

    16 large sea scallops
    3 tablespoons macadamia nut oil
    6 thin slices pancetta
    1 handful baby arugula
    1 small head butter lettuce, torn into large pieces
    1 teaspoon lemon zest
    2 tablespoons chopped fennel fronds
    2 teaspoons red wine vinegar
    salt

Preheat your grill to medium. Brush the scallops lightly with the oil. Cut the pancetta to fit around the scallops' rims. Wrap a strip of pancetta around each scallop. In a large stainless steel bowl, toss together the arugula, butter lettuce, lemon zest, and fennel. Sprinkle with the vinegar, and salt to taste. Mix thoroughly, and adjust seasonings as desired. Divide the salad among the four plates. Season the scallops with salt on both sides, and grill until the pancetta is crisp on the edges and the scallops are cooked through, about 5 to 8 minutes. Remove from the grill, and place on top of the salads.

Hedges Lane Ham Casserole

Yield: 6 servings   *Carbohydrates per serving: 7*

    1 medium cauliflower
    4 tablespoons butter
    1 cup heavy whipping cream
    4 ounces cheddar cheese, shredded
    ½ cup sour cream
    2 cups cubed cooked ham
    1 cup mushrooms, your choice, sliced
    1 cup parmesan cheese, grated
    1 tablespoon cold butter

Cut cauliflower into florets, and cook in boiling salted water for about 10 minutes or until tender; drain and set aside. Melt the 4 tablespoons of butter in a medium saucepan over medium heat. Do not let it burn. Slowly add the heavy cream, whisking constantly until the mixture starts to reduce and thicken slightly. Add the cheddar cheese and sour cream, stirring until the cheese melts, but do not let this boil. Stir the cauliflower, ham, and mushrooms into the cheese sauce, and pour into a 2-quart baking dish. Sprinkle the parmesan cheese evenly over the casserole. Cut 1 tablespoon of cold butter into pieces, and sprinkle over the parmesan. Bake uncovered in a preheated 350-degree F oven for 45 minutes.

Pecan Bacon-Wrapped Pork Tenderloin

Yield: 8 servings   *Carbohydrates per serving: 1*

    4 tablespoons macadamia nut oil
    ¾ pound of your favorite mushrooms, sliced
    1 small onion, chopped
    ¼ cup chopped pecans, toasted
    2 (12-ounce) pork tenderloins, flattened to ¼-inch thickness
    1 teaspoon salt
    1 teaspoon fresh ground black pepper
    8 thick bacon slices
    macadamia nut oil spray
    1 teaspoon fresh cracked black pepper

Heat the oil in a large skillet over medium-high heat, add the mush-rooms and onion, and sauté for 8 to 10 minutes or until tender. Stir in the pecans, and set aside. Flatten the pork loins or have the butcher do this for you, to ¼-inch thickness. To do this yourself, you'll need a rolling pin or a meat mallet. After flattening, sprinkle with salt and ground pepper. Spread the mushroom mixture evenly on one side of the tenderloin, leaving a ¼-inch border. Roll it up jellyroll-style, start-ing with the long end, and wrap 4 bacon slices around each tenderloin. Secure with toothpicks, and place on a lightly oil-sprayed rack in a roasting pan, seam sides down. Rub with the cracked pepper. Bake uncovered in a preheated 450-degree F oven for 15 minutes. Reduce the temperature to 400 degrees F, and cook for another 15 minutes.

Lower East Side Guacamole

Yield: 4 servings   *Carbohydrates per serving: 5*

    juice of 1 fresh lemon
    salt
    1 clove garlic, minced fine
    2 medium avocados, peeled
    1 cup fresh basil leaves, chopped
    ¼ cup scallions, finely diced
    2 heads Belgian endive
    sour cream, if desired

In a medium bowl, stir together the lemon juice, salt, and garlic. Add the avocados, and mash coarsely with a fork. Add the basil and scallions to the bowl, and mix together. Separate the endive leaves, and arrange four to a plate. Spoon the guacamole onto each endive leaf. Garnish with a dollop of sour cream, if desired.

Northwest Smoked Pork

Yield: 8 servings   *Carbohydrates per serving: 0*

This requires a lot of preparation time but makes for an elegant and out-of-the-ordinary barbecue.

2 cups prepared mustard
¾ cup white wine vinegar
1 tablespoon hot sauce
2 tablespoons macadamia nut oil
1 (5–6 pound) pork butt roast
5 garlic cloves, chopped
2 tablespoons salt
1 tablespoon pepper

Soak hickory or mesquite wood chips in water for 1 hour.

Cook the mustard, vinegar, hot sauce, and oil in a large saucepan over low heat, stirring often, for about 20 minutes. Remove from heat and set aside. Cut several deep slits in the roast. Stir together the garlic, salt, and pepper, and rub on the roast. I usually rub the roast with macadamia nut oil before doing this step, to get it nice and wet so that the seasonings really stick and make the dish quite pungent. Prepare your smoker, and let the fire burn for 15 to 20 minutes. Drain the wood, and place on the coals. Place water pan in the smoker, and add water to the fill line. Place the roast in the center of the lower food rack, and pour 1 cup of the mustard mixture over the roast. Cook covered with the smoker lid for 6 to 7 hours, adding additional wood and charcoal as needed. Remove the roast from the smoker and allow to cool slightly. Chop, and serve with the remaining mustard sauce.

TexMex Tuna Melts

Yield: 4 servings   *Carbohydrates per serving: 2*

This dish is quite impressive because you are making it with fresh tuna, not canned.

> 4 (4-ounce) fresh tuna fillets
> macadamia nut oil spray
> 2 celery ribs, peeled and chopped on the diagonal
> ½ teaspoon ground chipotle pepper
> ½ teaspoon chili powder
> 3 tablespoons Maconnaise (see recipe on page 205)
> 2 tablespoons Dijon mustard
> 2 teaspoons lime juice
> pepper, to taste
> salt, to taste
> 4 slices swiss cheese (1 ounce)

Spray the tuna fillets with oil and grill them on a heated grill, about 4 minutes per side or until desired doneness. Depending on your guests, you may need to make individual tuna salads. Mix together the celery, Maconnaise, chipotle and chili peppers, mustard, and lime juice. Shred the tuna fillets, and mix into the Maconnaise mixture. Add salt and pepper to taste. Divide into 4 equal portions, and place on an aluminum foil–lined cookie sheet. Lay one slice of cheese over each mound of tuna salad. Broil 6 inches from the heat for about 5 minutes or until the cheese melts.

Variations

You may use canned tuna, in case the tuna is not fresh at the market that day. Another variation is *Salmon Melts*. These are prepared the exact same way as the previous recipe, and you may use either fresh (preferable) or canned wild salmon.

Roast Beef with Melted Provolone Roll-Ups

1 pound thinly sliced roast beef
4 slices provolone cheese
horseradish
salt and pepper to taste

On a cookie sheet, divide the roast beef into 4 equal portions. Lay a slice of provolone cheese onto each bed of roast beef and spread with horseradish. Sprinkle with salt and pepper. Roll up, and secure with toothpicks that have been sitting in a water bath for 30 minutes. Place in a preheated 375-degree F oven until the cheese melts, about 5 to 8 minutes, and serve.

Entrees

Mama's Stuffed Green Peppers

Yield: 6 servings   *Carbohydrates per serving: 6*

This dish can be a side dish vegetable, as recommended in the menu section, or it can be a main course by itself. The recipe was handed down to me from my mother so it's very dear to my heart. It was actually one of the few low-carbohydrate dishes she ever made. Of course, it was served with pasta, but we won't suggest that here.

6 medium-size Italian green frying peppers
1 pound ground chuck
1 medium onion, minced fine
2 cloves garlic, minced
¼ teaspoon crushed red pepper
½ teaspoon salt
½ teaspoon pepper
1 cup shredded parmesan cheese
macadamia nut oil, as needed

Cut the tops off the peppers, and remove the innards, including the seeds. Cook ground beef in a large skillet over medium heat, about 6 minutes, stirring until the beef crumbles. Add the onion and garlic, and sauté 4 more minutes or until the beef is no longer pink. Remove from heat and drain. Stir in the crushed red pepper, salt, and black pepper.

Spoon the mixture evenly into the frying peppers, and place in a baking dish that has been lightly coated with oil. Sprinkle the parmesan cheese over the peppers, lightly drizzle some macadamia nut oil on top, and place in a preheated 350-degree F oven for about 30 minutes. Check them after about 20 minutes to make sure the peppers get soft but do not burn on the top. Cover with foil, if needed, at this time.

Daddy's Meatballs

Yield: 6 servings   *Carbohydrates per serving: 2*

I must give credit where it is due. My mother was a great cook, but she had nothing over my dad, who was always in the kitchen on the weekends, working alongside my mother or pushing her out of the way to get to the stove. These are his creations, and they're delicious.

½ pound ground veal
½ pound ground pork
½ pound ground chuck
1 teaspoon kosher salt
½ teaspoon crushed red pepper
½ teaspoon coarsely ground black pepper
2 ounces grated parmesan cheese
2 teaspoons chopped fresh tarragon
2 teaspoons chopped fresh basil—preferably from your own garden
1 egg
macadamia nut oil—enough for frying

In a large porcelain bowl, mix well all the ingredients except the oil with your hands. Using your palms, roll the mixture into 1-inch balls, and place on a dish. Do this until the meat mixture has been fully used up. In a large cast-iron skillet, pour oil to a depth of about ¼ inch. Be generous. Heat over high heat, and when the oil is heated, place the meatballs about ½ inch apart, filling the skillet. Sauté and brown on each side, turning to cook all sides evenly. Once you place the meatballs in the skillet, the temperature of the oil will come down. Keep the heat on high until the oil starts to heat again, then lower it to medium high so that the meatballs cook through and don't burn. When cooked, remove to paper towels and drain. Divide into 6 portions, and serve.

Curried Beef

Yield: 4 servings   *Carbohydrates per serving: 0*

1 pound flank steak, trimmed
4 tablespoons macadamia nut oil
½ cup green onions, sliced
1 clove garlic, minced
1 tablespoon ground coriander
1 teaspoon ground cumin
½ teaspoon salt
¼ teaspoon turmeric
½ cup red wine

Cut steak diagonally across the grain into thin slices. Heat the oil in a large skillet, add onions and garlic, and sauté for 5 minutes until onions are translucent. Add the coriander, cumin, salt, and turmeric, and sauté for another minute. Add the steak, and cook for about 5 to 7 minutes. Add red wine, and simmer for 3 more minutes or until thoroughly heated.

Milanese Shrimp

Yield: 6 servings   *Carbohydrates per serving: 1*

1 small red onion
2 cloves garlic, peeled
1 pound medium shrimp, peeled, deveined, and butterflied
1 cup loosely packed fresh farm-stand basil
sea salt
crushed red pepper
1 tablespoon red wine vinegar
¼ cup macadamia nut oil

Slice the red onion so that the slices are almost transparent. Season and set aside. Bring water to a boil in a large pot, add the garlic and the shrimp, and cook for about 3 minutes, until just done—do not overcook. Drain the shrimp and submerge in an ice bath to stop the cooking process. In a large stainless steel bowl, combine the basil, onion, salt, and pepper. Add the shrimp and vinegar, and mix together gently. Add the oil and mix again, until everything is combined through and the basil is wilted. Taste, and adjust the seasonings.

Kobe Short Ribs

Yield: 4 servings   *Carbohydrates per serving: 2*

This takes preparation time.

- ¾ cup lite soy sauce
- ½ cup macadamia nut oil
- 3 small serrano chilies, stemmed, seeded, and sliced thinly
- 5 green onions, trimmed and sliced thinly (leave the green on)
- 1 garlic clove, minced
- 1-inch piece fresh ginger, peeled and finely minced
- 4 pounds short ribs
- ¼ cup sesame seeds, toasted
- 2 tablespoons fresh cilantro, minced

In a large stainless steel bowl, mix the soy sauce, oil, chilies, green onions, garlic, and ginger. Add the ribs, and toss well to coat. Cover and marinate overnight in the refrigerator, turning every time you remember. Remove meat from the marinade, and pour the marinade into a saucepan over high heat. Bring to a boil; reduce heat to medium, and simmer uncovered for about 5 minutes until thickened. Place ribs in a shallow roasting pan, bone side down, and bake until tender in a 375-degree F preheated oven, about 45 minutes to 1 hour, depending on thickness. Baste every 15 minutes with the cooked marinade. Alternatively, these may be grilled over a low heat for 1 to 1½ hours. When they're done, remove to plates, drizzle with marinade once again, sprinkle with the toasted sesame seeds and cilantro, and serve.

Baked Eggplant Slices with Parmesan

Yield: 4 servings   *Carbohydrates per serving: 6*

1 (1½-pound) eggplant
macadamia nut oil—for coating
kosher salt
crushed black pepper
fresh-squeezed lemon juice
¾ cup freshly grated parmesan cheese

Cut the eggplant into ½-inch-thick slices, and place on a baking sheet. Rub each side with the oil; season with salt and pepper and a squeeze of lemon juice. Pour half the parmesan cheese over the eggplant, and place in a preheated 400-degree F oven for 6 minutes. Turn over, sprinkle the remaining parmesan cheese on the eggplant, and cook for another 4 minutes. For the remaining 3 minutes, turn the heat up to 500 degrees F until the parmesan is browned. Remove from heat, and serve immediately.

Mecox Lamb Burgers

Yield: 4 servings   *Carbohydrates per serving: 2*

1 pound ground lamb
large handful of fresh cilantro, chopped fine
large handful of fresh mint leaves, minced fine
½ red onion, chopped into a fine dice
1 small red chili, finely diced
½ teaspoon ground cumin
1 cup crumbled feta cheese
raw spinach leaves

In a stainless steel bowl, combine all the ingredients, except the cheese, until mixed well. Form this mixture into 8 hamburger patties. Press an equal amount of cheese on 4 of the patties, and cover with the other 4. Seal the edges with your fingers, and refrigerate. On a pre-heated medium-high grill, sear each side for 3 to 4 minutes for medium or until desired doneness. Serve on a bed of spinach leaves.

Variation

Turkey may be substituted as the meat for another meal.

Fiery Escolar with Tabasco and Horseradish

Yield: 6 servings   *Carbohydrates per serving: 1*

This is a recipe adapted from Doug Rodriguez.

   1½ pounds skinless escolar fillet
   ½ cup fresh-squeezed lime juice
   1 tablespoon sea salt

For the marinade:

   1 tablespoon lite soy sauce
   ½ cup fresh-squeezed lime juice
   1 tablespoon Tabasco sauce
   1 teaspoon horseradish
   ¼ cup coarsely chopped cilantro for garnish

Cut the fish into large rectangular pieces, each about 2 inches. Set on a baking sheet, cover with plastic wrap, and freeze for 1 to 2 hours, until firm but not solid. Once frozen, remove from freezer and slice each piece crosswise very thin. In a stainless steel bowl, combine the fish, lime juice, and salt. Cover, and refrigerate for 2 hours. When ready to serve, drain the fish, and discard the lime juice. In a clean stainless steel bowl, blend the marinade ingredients together, and gently toss in the fish and the garnish. Refrigerate for 1 hour before serving.

   For those of you who don't know this, you can cook fish with lemon or lime juice without cooking it in the oven. That is the trick behind ceviches. This is not sushi—the fish is not raw but is cured by the acid in the lemon or lime juice.

Settler's Stuffed Mushrooms

Yield: 4 servings   *Carbohydrates per serving: 4*

3 tablespoons macadamia nut oil, plus more for brushing
1 green onion, finely diced
3 garlic cloves, chopped
large handful of fresh basil leaves, chopped
¾ pound boiled shrimp, chopped; or shredded crabmeat
4 tablespoons freshly grated parmesan cheese
4 ounces fresh chevre
2 ounces cream cheese
chipotle pepper
sea salt
20 cremini mushrooms, stems removed
parsley for garnish

Over medium-high heat, heat the oil in a large skillet. Add the onion and garlic, and sauté for about 5 minutes until the onion softens. Add the basil, and sauté for another minute. Transfer to a medium stainless steel bowl, and mix in the remaining ingredients, except for the mushrooms. Season to taste. Lightly brush each mushroom cap with oil, and place on a baking dish. Mound the filling into each cap, pressing to ensure it stays intact. Bake in a preheated 350-degree F oven for about 25 minutes or until golden brown on top. Place 5 mushrooms on each plate, and garnish with a sprig of parsley. Please note that the filling can be made ahead of time and refrigerated until needed.

Simple Roast Chicken with Fresh Herbs

Yield: 4 servings   *Carbohydrates per serving: 0*

Serves 4

4 chicken breast halves with rib in
4 tablespoons macadamia nut oil
1 teaspoon fresh rosemary, chopped
1 teaspoon fresh tarragon leaves, chopped
1 teaspoon fresh dill, chopped
1 teaspoon fresh chervil, chopped
salt and pepper to taste
1 lemon, cut into quarters

Preheat the oven to 475 degrees F. Put all the ingredients except chicken in a medium stainless steel bowl, and mix together well. Put the chicken in a roasting pan, squeeze the lemon quarters over the chicken, and pour the herb mixture over the chicken. Add the squeezed lemon rinds to pan for a richer flavor. Place in the oven, and lower the temperature to 425 degrees F. Cook chicken for 35 to 45 minutes, turning once. Chicken is cooked when firm or when juices run clear.

Spicy Grilled Steak

Yield: 4 servings   *Carbohydrates per serving: 0*

This requires advance preparation time.

　　4 cloves garlic, peeled
　　2 cups packed fresh parsley
　　1½ cups macadamia nut oil
　　¼ cup red wine vinegar
　　2 tablespoons fresh chopped basil
　　2 teaspoons ground cumin
　　2 teaspoons sea salt
　　1 teaspoon crushed red pepper
　　two 1-pound pieces of flank steak, pounded
　　fresh ground black pepper
　　salt to taste

Combine the first 8 ingredients in a food processor, and process until well blended. Place meat in a large glass baking dish. Season with salt and pepper. Brush meat on both sides with the sauce. Cover, and refrigerate for at least 3 hours. This can be prepared the night before. Prepare a hot fire on the grill, or turn grill to high. Grill about 3 minutes per side. Do not overcook, as flank steak can become quite tough if overcooked. If there is a flare-up, remove the steak and wait for the flare-up to subside. Transfer to a cutting board, and let sit for 5 minutes. Cut each steak against the grain at an angle into very thin slices. Dollop some of the sauce over each serving, and put the remainder into small bowls for additional dipping, as needed. If you wish to broil the steak, broil about 4 minutes on each side and do not overcook.

Creole Rubbed Tuna Steak

Yield: 4 servings   *Carbohydrates per serving: 0*

This takes advance preparation time.

   4 (8-ounce) tuna fillets
   1 tablespoon curry powder
   4 tablespoons macadamia nut oil
   2 tablespoons minced fresh garlic
   1 Scotch bonnet pepper, stemmed, seeded, and minced
   1 teaspoon grated fresh ginger
   sea salt
   freshly ground coarse black pepper
   arugula leaves (raw)

Combine all the ingredients except arugula in a stainless steel bowl, and mix together until the tuna steaks are well coated. Refrigerate for 2 hours. On a preheated grill over high heat, sear the tuna on each side for 2 minutes. This will leave the tuna seared on the outside but raw on the inside. For more doneness, cook on each side for an additional minute until it reaches the desired temperature. Serve over a bed of arugula leaves.

Cross Grilled Pork Chops with Pico de Gallo

Yield: 8 servings   *Carbohydrates per serving: 3*

This requires advance preparation time.

   2 teaspoons garlic powder
   2 teaspoons fennel seed, crushed
   1 teaspoon achiote
   1 teaspoon black pepper
   1 teaspoon cayenne pepper
   1 teaspoon crushed red pepper
   1 teaspoon chipotle pepper
   1 teaspoon oregano
   1 teaspoon kosher salt
   2 tablespoons macadamia nut oil, plus more to coat the grill
   8 center-cut pork chops (4 to 6 ounces each)

Mix the spices together well in a stainless steel bowl. Pour in the oil, add the pork chops, and mix until the chops are well coated with the seasonings and the oil. Massage in the seasonings, and marinate chops for at least 1 hour. I often marinate them overnight. Preheat your grill to medium-high. Remove the grilling rack, and oil it. Once the fire is ready, place the oiled grilling rack back over the heat and allow it to heat. Cook the chops on each side, about 5 minutes for medium to medium rare. Cook equally on each side for more doneness. Serve with pico de gallo.

Weekend Halibut

Yield: 4 servings   *Carbohydrates per serving: 0*

> 3 tablespoons coriander seeds
> 1 tablespoon salt
> 3 tablespoons macadamia nut oil
> ½ cup macadamia nut oil
> 2 pounds halibut fillets
> 2 tablespoons fresh-squeezed lime juice
> ¼ cup chopped fresh cilantro
> ½ red onion, minced

Over high heat, sauté the coriander seeds until they begin to pop, about 4 minutes. Crush the seeds and the salt, and blend in with the 3 tablespoons of oil. Set aside. Put the fish fillets and the rest of the ingredients in a stainless steel bowl, and allow to marinate for less than 1 hour. Heat the grill to medium, and cook the fillets on each side for 3 minutes or so, depending on thickness and desired doneness. Evenly divide onto plates, and drizzle the coriander oil over each fillet.

Hayground Grilled Steak with Chipotle and Bacon

Yield: 4 servings   *Carbohydrates per serving: 2*

4 tablespoons macadamia nut oil
8 strips of bacon, cut into small pieces
1 small white onion, chopped into a fine dice
2 chipotle peppers, seeded, peeled, and minced
1 cup beef broth, organic, low sodium
2 pounds filet mignon
kosher salt
crushed black pepper
crushed chipotle pepper

In a medium saucepan, heat the oil over medium heat. Add the bacon and cook until crisp, turning occasionally. Add the onion, and sauté for 5 minutes until it softens. Lower the heat, and add the chipotle and the broth, and allow to gently simmer and reduce. Season the filet mignon with the salt and two peppers, and preheat your grill as hot as it will go. Grill the meat on both sides for about 4 minutes for medium rare. Continue to cook evenly on each side if more doneness is desired. Allow the meat to sit for 10 minutes, then cut across the grain, and divide evenly among four plates. Pour the sauce over each steak, and serve with your favorite salad and vegetable.

Wain's Rack of Lamb

Yield: 6 servings   *Carbohydrates per serving: 1*

1 cup Italian parsley
1 cup fresh mint leaves
2 teaspoons capers
2 ounces macadamia nuts
¾ cup macadamia nut oil
2 teaspoons white wine vinegar
sea salt
coarse ground black pepper
crushed red pepper
4 racks of lamb with 4 ribs each

In a food processor, mix together the parsley and mint. Add the capers and nuts, and combine with the herbs. With the processor on, pour the oil in slowly to combine. Add the vinegar, and season with the salt and two peppers. When fully combined, rub the backs of the racks along the bone with the sauce, using your fingers. Save the rest to serve as a sauce. Place the racks in a roasting pan into a preheated 425-degree F oven for about 35 minutes for medium rare. If you're using a meat thermometer, medium rare is 130 degrees.

Bayou Catfish with Vegetables and Basil

Yield: 4 servings   *Carbohydrates per serving: 6*

6 tablespoons macadamia nut oil
8 ounces snow pea pods
1 green onion, white part only, minced
1 green bell pepper, chopped
½ teaspoon salt
½ teaspoon pepper
1 tablespoon creole seasoning (make sure it doesn't have sugar)
four 6- to 8-ounce catfish fillets
½ cup heavy whipping cream
2 tablespoons chopped fresh basil

Place 3 tablespoons of oil in a large skillet, and heat over medium-high heat. Add the pea pods, onion, and chopped peppers. Sauté for 5 minutes or until just tender. Stir in the salt and pepper for another minute, allowing the flavors to seal, then transfer to a serving dish and keep warm. In the same skillet pour the remaining oil, and heat it over medium-high heat. Once the oil is hot, cook the fillets 2 to 3 minutes on each side or until desired doneness. Divide the vegetable mixture onto 4 plates, and place one fillet on top of each pile of vegetables. Then add the cream to the skillet, stirring to loosen the particles from the bottom of the skillet. Add the chopped basil and creole seasoning and cook, stirring often, about 3 to 5 minutes or until thickened. The longer you reduce this, the thicker it will become. Pour the sauce over the fish, and serve.

Flying Point Stuffed Cheeseburger

Yield: 4 servings   *Carbohydrates per serving: 4*

3 tablespoons macadamia nut oil
¾ pound cremini mushrooms, chopped
1 garlic clove, minced fine
½ onion, minced fine
2 tablespoons chicken stock
kosher salt
freshly ground black pepper
1 pound 85% lean ground beef (chuck)
1 cup Gruyere cheese
spinach leaves (raw)

In a medium-sized skillet, heat the oil over medium-high heat. Then, put the mushrooms in the skillet and cook for 1 minute, stirring frequently. Add the garlic, onion, and the chicken stock, and cook, stirring constantly, for about 7 minutes or until the mushrooms have sweated completely and the juices have evaporated. Season with salt and pepper. Set aside to cool completely. In a stainless steel bowl, combine the beef and cheese, and mix well. Form this mixture into 8 hamburger patties. Press an equal amount of the mushroom stuffing on 4 of the patties, and cover with the other 4. Seal the edges with your fingers, and refrigerate. On a preheated medium-high grill, sear each side for 3 to 4 minutes for medium or until desired doneness. Serve on a bed of spinach leaves.

Other Variations for Stuffings

Italian: Use 1 cup mozzarella cheese and ¼ cup fresh basil pesto.

Western: Use 2 strips cooked bacon, crumbled, and 1 cup cheddar cheese.

Abraham's Curried Chicken

Yield: 4 servings   *Carbohydrates per serving: 4*

3 pounds chicken thighs or whole roasting chicken, cut into pieces
sea salt
freshly ground black pepper
½ cup macadamia nut oil
1 green onion, white part only, chopped
4 garlic cloves, peeled
3 tablespoons fresh ginger, roughly chopped
1 tablespoon ground cumin
1 teaspoon ground coriander
2 fresh red chilies
1 tablespoon lite soy sauce
1 (11-ounce) can unsweetened coconut milk
2 limes
½ cup fresh cilantro, chopped

Season the chicken with salt and pepper. Heat the oil in a large skillet over medium-high heat, and brown the chicken for 15 to 20 minutes, turning once. Combine the onion, garlic, ginger, cumin, and coriander in a food processor. Add the fresh chilies and the soy sauce, and combine well. Pulse in half the coconut milk to form a thick paste. Remove the chicken from the skillet and discard most of the oil, leaving only a thin film. Add the curry paste you've just made, and cook over medium heat for about 2 minutes, stirring frequently so that it doesn't burn. Add the remaining coconut milk, and bring to a boil. Put the chicken and any juices back into the skillet, and cook uncovered until the chicken is tender, about 35 minutes. Juice one lime, and stir into the mixture. Quarter the other lime, and set aside. Divide the chicken among four plates, and garnish with chopped cilantro and lime quarters.

Playhouse Snapper Stew

Yield: 4 servings   *Carbohydrates per serving: 6*

2 pounds snapper fillets
2 tablespoons macadamia nut oil
1 head garlic, each clove peeled and finely chopped
one 4-inch piece of lemongrass, finely chopped
4 Thai chilies, seeded and finely chopped
2 shallots, peeled and cut into a fine dice
1 quart chicken broth
2 tablespoons fresh-squeezed lime juice
¼ cup chunky unsweetened peanut butter
1 (11-ounce) can unsweetened coconut milk
2 tablespoons fresh basil leaves, finely chopped
large bunch of cilantro, finely chopped

Cut the fish into 1-inch strips, and set aside in the refrigerator. Heat the oil in a deep cast-iron skillet over medium heat, and sauté the garlic, lemongrass, chilies, and shallots for about 5 minutes. Add the chicken broth and lime juice, and bring to a slow simmer. Whisk the peanut butter into this mixture until well blended. Stir in the fish and the coconut milk, and simmer gently until the fish is light and flaky, about 2 minutes. Stir in the basil and cilantro, simmer for another 2 minutes, and serve.

Tuscan Grilled Steak

Yield: 6 servings   *Carbohydrates per serving: 2*

3 pounds sirloin steak, about 2 inches thick
1 cup radicchio, shredded
2 ounces parmesan cheese, shaved

Grill the steak on a high heat, about 5 minutes per side for medium rare. Transfer to a cutting board, and let sit for 10 minutes. Slice against the grain, diagonally, and arrange on a serving plate. Cover with shredded radicchio, and top with parmesan shavings.

Montauk Shrimp in Gansett Green Sauce

Yield: 4 servings   *Carbohydrates per serving: 3*

6 cloves garlic
⅓ cup macadamia nut oil
6 scallions, trimmed and chopped
1 cup parsley leaves
2 pounds shrimp, peeled and deveined (14–16 count)
salt
pepper
4 dried chilies, crushed
⅓ cup fish stock or water

Combine garlic and oil in a food processor, and blend until smooth. Add the scallions and parsley, and pulse until mixture is minced. Toss with shrimp, salt, pepper, and chilies. Put the shrimp mixture into a roasting pan, add the liquid, and place in a preheated 500-degree F oven. Roast for about 10 minutes or until the mixture is bubbly hot and the shrimp are pink.

Korean Spiced Fried Chicken

Yield: 4 servings   *Carbohydrates per serving: 0*

crushed pork rinds
½ teaspoon red chili pepper
½ teaspoon ground cumin
½ teaspoon ground chipotle pepper
6 chicken breast halves, rib and skin on
¾ cup heavy cream
macadamia nut oil for frying

Combine the pork rinds and spices together in a shallow dish. Pour the cream into a small bowl. Dip the chicken breast into the cream, then coat thoroughly with the spice mixture on both sides. Place on a clean plate. In a large cast-iron skillet, heat 2 inches of oil until 375 degrees F. If you don't have a thermometer, the oil is hot when a pork rind placed in the oil sizzles. Place chicken breasts in the oil and cook until done, about 35 to 40 minutes, depending on their size, turning once.

Mill Creek Lobster

Yield: 6 servings   *Carbohydrates per serving: 2*

Please note that this recipe works with any shellfish you desire, such as shrimp, crabmeat, or even crayfish.

    4 tablespoons macadamia nut oil
    4 cloves garlic, chopped finely
    1 pound lobster meat
    2 teaspoons red wine
    ½ pound fresh ground pork
    2 teaspoons lite soy sauce
    sea salt
    ground fresh black pepper
    2 cups chicken or fish stock
    2 eggs, lightly beaten
    2 scallions, white part only, sliced fine on a diagonal

Heat 1 tablespoon of the oil in a large skillet. When the oil is hot, add 2 cloves of garlic and cook until lightly browned, about 8 minutes. Add the lobster, and stir fry; add 1 tablespoon of red wine, and continue to sauté. When the lobster is hot, set aside. Pour the remaining oil into another skillet, heat, then add the remaining garlic and the pork and sauté until the pork is cooked through. Add the rest of the wine, soy sauce, pepper, and stock, and bring to a boil. Heat over high heat to reduce the liquid for about 2 minutes. Lower the heat to medium, and stir in the eggs, letting them cook for about 30 seconds, and then fold with a spoon. Return the lobster to the skillet, and stir the mixture slightly. Sprinkle with the scallions and another drizzle of oil, and serve.

Rosemary Grilled Flanken

Yield: 6 servings   *Carbohydrates per serving: 0*

This recipe requires advance preparation time.

½ cup macadamia nut oil
2 tablespoons chopped fresh parsley
2 bay leaves
2 green onions, chopped fine
3 garlic cloves, minced
1 bunch fresh basil, chopped fine
1 teaspoon salt
½ teaspoon crushed red pepper
2 pounds flank steak
2 tablespoons fresh-squeezed lemon juice
fresh rosemary sprigs

Combine the first eight ingredients into a bowl, and reserve ⅓ of the mixture. Place the steak in a shallow dish, and pour the mixture over it. Cover and chill for 2 to 4 hours, turning occasionally. Remove the steak from the marinade, discard marinade. Grill over a medium-high heat, covered, for 8 to 10 minutes on each side or to desired degree of doneness, brushing with the reserved marinade. Cut steak diagonally across the grain into thin strips, squeeze the lemon juice onto the steaks before serving, and garnish with a rosemary sprig.

Variation

Substitute lamb or pork chops, and treat the same. For pork chops, the cooking time will have to be a little longer, perhaps 12 minutes on each side, being careful not to overcook the pork. For lamb chops, the cooking time is a little less, about 4 to 6 minutes per side.

Flying Point Scallops with Bacon

Yield: 4 servings   *Carbohydrates per serving: 1*

This recipe was adapted from one created by chef Douglas Rodriguez. This takes advance preparation time.

16 diver scallops
¾ cup freshly squeezed lime juice
1 tablespoon sea salt
3 tablespoons fresh chopped chives
½ red onion, thinly sliced
3 serrano chilies, thinly sliced
½ cup chopped mint leaves
½ cup macadamia nut oil
½ pound cooked smoked bacon, crumbled

Set the scallops on a parchment paper–lined baking sheet, cover with plastic wrap, and freeze for 1 hour but not longer. Remove from the freezer two at a time, and slice into very thin rounds. In a stainless steel bowl, mix the rest of the ingredients together (except for the bacon). Gently toss the scallops in the mixture, and refrigerate for 2 hours until the scallops have a whitish, opaque appearance. When ready to serve, plate, and garnish with the bacon crumbles.

Beef Tenderloin with Provençal Maconnaise

Yield: 4 servings   *Carbohydrates per serving: 0*

This requires some advance preparation.

4 (8-ounce) beef tenderloins
macadamia oil—enough for marinade
1 teaspoon achiote
2 cloves garlic, minced
2 teaspoons chili powder
1 teaspoon crushed red pepper
kosher salt
pepper
½ cup red wine or beef stock

In a glass dish, pour some oil over the tenderloins, add the rest of the ingredients, and rub until the tenderloins are well coated. Marinate for at least 2 hours. When you are ready to cook, coat the bottom of a large cast-iron skillet well with macadamia nut oil, and let it get very hot over high heat. When the oil is hot, but not before, put the tenderloins in and sear each side. When they are seared, remove the skillet and place it in a 425-degree F oven for 15 minutes. Remove beef from the skillet, and allow to rest for 5 minutes. Put the skillet back on the stove, and over high heat, pour ½ cup red wine or beef stock and scrape the bottom of the skillet to make a nice reduction. Slice the beef, plate it, and pour the reduction over the tenderloin. Place a dollop of Provençal Maconnaise in the center of each plate, and serve.

Chicken Breast Pescatore

Yield: 4 servings   *Carbohydrates per serving: 1*

This is a variation on my favorite meal as a child—chicken cutlets. Since I no longer use breading, I have found that parmesan cheese works just as well, although it's a little saltier.

    1 teaspoon cayenne pepper
    2 cups freshly grated parmesan
    2 eggs
    ½ cup heavy cream
    kosher salt
    freshly ground black pepper
    macadamia oil for frying
    2 pounds chicken breasts, boneless and skinless, pounded thin

Combine the cayenne and the parmesan on a plate. Beat eggs in a bowl with the heavy cream, salt, and pepper. In a large skillet, pour oil to a depth of about ¼ inch. Dip the breasts into the parmesan, then into the egg, and then back into the parmesan. Place on another plate until each breast has been coated. Heat the oil on medium-high heat, and do not put the chicken in it until the oil is very hot. You'll know when it's ready if you drop a small piece of the parmesan coating into the oil, and it begins to sizzle. This is the key to making chicken cutlets without breading: the oil must be hot. Place the chicken cutlets in the oil, and allow to cook thoroughly on the first side before turning. They are not ready to turn until the side facing you starts to look as if it's cooking. Gingerly, with a spatula, turn the chicken and allow to cook until this side appears golden brown. Remove to a plate and serve.

Swordfish à la Woodsfield

Yield: 4 servings   *Carbohydrates per serving: 0*

  1½ pounds swordfish steak, cubed
  3 ancho chilies
  zest of one lime
  sea salt
  1½ cups macadamia nut oil
  juice of one lime, freshly squeezed
  freshly ground black pepper

Arrange the fish in a single layer in a roasting pan. Sprinkle with the chilies, lime zest, and salt. Pour enough oil to just lightly cover the fish, cover with foil, and place in a 225-degree F oven. Bake until swordfish is just done, about 40 minutes, depending on desired doneness. Allow fish to cool in pan. Remove fish from pan to plate, drizzle with lime juice, and crack salt and pepper over each plate.

White Sands Pork Shoulder

Yield: 4 to 6 servings   *Carbohydrates per serving: 1*

  one 3½-pound pork shoulder
  kosher salt
  freshly ground black pepper
  3 tablespoons macadamia nut oil
  ½ cup veal or beef stock, plus more if needed
  5 large cloves garlic, with skin left on, crushed
  1 leek, with larger greener leaves removed, diced
  4 celery stalks, peeled and trimmed, diced finely on the diagonal
  10 sprigs fresh thyme
  4 sprigs fresh parsley, coarsely chopped
  1 bay leaf
  ½ cup dry red wine

Season the pork generously with salt and pepper. In a large cast-iron skillet, heat about 3 tablespoons of oil until very hot, then sear the pork shoulder on all sides until browned evenly. In a large roasting dish or casserole, add the stock and the garlic, leek, celery, and herbs. Sauté over medium-high heat until the vegetables are soft and the stock has reduced, about 3 minutes. Lay the pork on top of the vegetables, and add more stock to cover the bottom half of the pork. Cover the pan with foil, and place in a 325-degree F preheated oven. Braise the pork for the next 2½ hours, being certain to turn it about once every half-hour. Baste with the juices. The turning is important, so that the meat braises evenly. When the pork is done, remove, and let sit for at least 20 minutes. Slice, and arrange on a serving platter. Strain the pan juices into a small saucepan, add the red wine, and heat to boiling. I always let it boil for a few minutes to remove the alcohol and to get a thicker reduction. Pour over the pork, and serve.

Shad Roast on a Bed of Radish, Celery, and Fennel

Yield: 4 servings   *Carbohydrates per serving: 2*

3 ribs of celery, with the stringy outer part removed, cut thin at an angle
6 radishes, sliced into thin rounds
1 cup of flat-leaf parsley (outer leaves only)
1 bulb fennel, sliced thin
½ red onion, sliced thin
2 tablespoons lime juice, freshly squeezed
4 tablespoons macadamia nut oil, plus more for brushing
salt
pepper
four 6-ounce shad fillets

Put all salad ingredients in a stainless steel bowl, and dress with the lime juice, 4 tablespoons of oil, and salt and pepper to taste. Mix well, and allow to marinate. Meanwhile, season the shad fillets with salt and pepper; brush them lightly with the oil on both sides, then place the fillets on a hot grill and cook 5 to 6 minutes per side, depending on thickness and preferred degree of doneness. To serve, simply divide the marinated salad evenly among 4 serving plates, and place one portion of grilled fish atop each. This recipe can also be done in the oven at 350 degrees F for 10 minutes, turning once.

Chicken Devon

Yield: 4 servings   *Carbohydrates per serving: 1*

3 tablespoons macadamia nut oil
4 boneless, skinless chicken breast halves, flattened
kosher salt
fresh ground white pepper
1 shallot, chopped
1 tablespoon fresh chopped tarragon
½ cup heavy whipping cream
fresh-squeezed lemon juice, to taste
chopped fresh Italian parsley for garnish

Heat the oil in a large skillet over medium-high heat. Season the chicken with salt and pepper. When the oil is heated, add the chicken and sauté gently on each side, turning once, until the juices run clear, about 3 minutes per side. Transfer to a heated plate, and place in a food warmer. Pour off any excess fat from the skillet, and return to medium heat. Add the shallot, and sauté for about 1½ minutes. Add the tarragon and the cream, increase the heat, and stir, getting the browned bits on the bottom of the pan. Blend well. Continue stirring until mixture is bubbling, about 3 minutes. Do not burn. Sauce should be starting to thicken by this time. Season with salt, pepper, and a squeeze of lemon juice. Return the chicken to the pan, and coat well on each side. Put on individual plates, and lightly drizzle sauce over each breast. Sprinkle with the fresh parsley, and serve.

Down-Home Brisket with Texas Pecan Cilantro Pesto

Yield: 6 servings   *Carbohydrates per serving: 3*

1 (4-pound) brisket
macadamia nut oil for rubbing
2 tablespoons chili powder
1 tablespoon chipotle pepper powder or flakes
2 tablespoons kosher salt
1 tablespoon garlic powder
1 tablespoon onion powder
1 tablespoon freshly ground black pepper
2 tablespoons dry mustard
1 bay leaf, crushed
1½ cups beef stock
water as needed

Rub the brisket with a liberal dose of the oil. Combine all the dry ingredients in a bowl, and rub on the brisket. Place in a roasting pan, and roast uncovered in a preheated 350-degree F oven for 1 hour. Add the beef stock and enough water so that there is ½ inch in the bottom of the pan. Cover tightly, reduce heat to 300 degrees F, and cook for 3 hours or until tender. Remove the meat, and let sit for 20 minutes before carving. Before carving, pour the juice from the pan over the brisket, then slice against the grain for best results. Plate, and serve with Texas Pecan Cilantro Pesto.

Texas Pecan Cilantro Pesto

2 cups tightly packed fresh cilantro
1 cup Texas pecans
6 garlic cloves
2 tablespoons fresh-squeezed lime juice
1 cup macadamia nut oil
1 teaspoon kosher salt
2 tablespoons fresh ground black pepper
½ pound parmesan cheese, shredded

Combine all ingredients except the cheese in a blender or food processor, and blend well. Remove to a small stainless steel bowl, and stir in the cheese. This can be made ahead of time and stored in the refrigerator until ready to use.

Vegetables and Side Dishes

Chilled Sesame Asparagus

Yield: 4 to 6 servings   *Carbohydrates per serving: 3*

    1½ pounds asparagus, trimmed and peeled
    4 tablespoons macadamia nut oil
    1 tablespoon rice vinegar
    1 teaspoon soy sauce (lite, without sugar)
    1 tablespoon sesame seeds, toasted

Cook the asparagus stalks in boiling water for about 4 to 5 minutes, making sure they are still crisp when you remove them from the heat. Place them in an ice bath immediately to stop the cooking process. Drain, cover, and place in the refrigerator for 2 hours.

When ready to serve, take the oil, vinegar, and soy sauce, and whisk together in a small beaker. Arrange the asparagus on a serving plate, and drizzle the dressing over the stalks. Sprinkle with the toasted sesame seeds, and serve.

Sesame Broccoli

Yield: 4 servings   *Carbohydrates per serving: 3*

This is the same as the previous recipe but is served hot. You will need 1 pound of fresh broccoli instead of the asparagus.

Follow the same instructions, but do not chill the broccoli. Toss it with the oil, vinegar, and soy sauce mixture, and serve.

Mohawk Spinach

Yield: 4 servings   *Carbohydrates per serving: 4*

    1 pound fresh spinach
    4 tablespoons macadamia nut oil
    1 clove garlic, minced
    kosher salt
    crushed red pepper flakes
    4 ounces paneer cheese

Remove the stems from the spinach, and wash and rinse thoroughly. Spinach is tough to clean, so I always do this a few times to make sure all the dirt is off, and the recipe won't taste sandy. In a large heavy skillet, heat the oil; add the garlic, and sauté for 1 minute. Add the spinach and cover, cooking over high heat until steam appears. Reduce the heat, and simmer until tender for about 5 minutes. Remove from heat, plate, season to taste with the salt and red pepper, and then sprinkle the paneer cheese over the spinach; pop into a 450-degree F oven for 2 minutes, and serve.

Southern Succotash

Yield: 4 servings   *Carbohydrates per serving: 4*

    4 tablespoons macadamia nut oil
    1 cup chopped okra
    1½ cups cooked lima beans
    1¾ cup cut green beans
    ¼ cup finely chopped scallion, both green and white parts
    ½ cup heavy whipping cream
    salt
    pepper

In a saucepan, heat the oil, stir in all the ingredients, and simmer until slightly thickened and heated through. Salt and pepper to taste.

Vegetable Medley à la Noyack

Yield: 6 servings   *Carbohydrates per serving: 8*

  1 pound brussels sprouts
  10 small baby zucchini
  4 small turnips
  8 baby leeks, trimmed and left whole
  ¼ cup macadamia nut oil
  kosher salt
  crushed red pepper flakes
  freshly ground black pepper

In a large bowl, toss the vegetables with the oil, salt, and two peppers. In a large shallow roasting pan, arrange the vegetables in a single layer. Place in a 425-degree F preheated oven for about 45 to 55 minutes or until tender and browned on the top.

Variation

Baked Summer Farm-Fresh Vegetables

Yield: 6 servings   *Carbohydrates per serving will be a little lower at 6.*

Simply use the previous recipe, but choose whatever vegetables are fresh at the farm stand that day. You may choose three different colors of peppers, eggplant, asparagus, different colors of zucchini, or green beans, and prepare as previously instructed. The only difference is that you may not need to cook them as long, if you strictly use summer vegetables, so check every 15 minutes. They will most likely be done in 30 minutes, depending on your assortment of fresh vegetables.

Double-Baked Sweet Potato with Cheddar and Bacon

Yield: 2 servings   *Carbohydrates per serving: 17*

  1 small to medium-sized sweet potato
  2 tablespoons butter
  2 ounces cheddar cheese, shredded
  2 pieces bacon, cooked and crumbled
  kosher salt
  fresh crushed black pepper

Cover the sweet potato with aluminum foil. Pierce the potato and foil in several different locations, and bake in a 425-degree F oven for 60 minutes or until tender. Remove and slice the potato in half lengthwise. Remove the insides of the potato, and place in a small bowl. Add the butter, cheese, and bacon, and mash together well. Season to taste, and spoon it back into the potato shell. Put back into the oven for 15 minutes or until the tops are browned.

Cauliflower au Gratin

Yield: 6 servings   *Carbohydrates per serving: 5*

    1 head cauliflower, cut into florets
    2 tablespoons heavy whipping cream
    4 ounces blue cheese
    4 slices bacon, cooked and crumbled

Boil the cauliflower in salted water until tender; drain. In a bowl, using a hand mixer, thoroughly grind the cauliflower until it has the consistency of mashed potatoes. Add the cream, and mix well. Place in a buttered casserole dish, sprinkle the cheese and bacon on top, and cook in a preheated 375-degree F oven for 30 minutes.

Hint: Pureed cauliflower makes a great thickening agent for soups or sauces.

Job's Okra

Yield: 4 servings   *Carbohydrates per serving: 5*

    ½ cup peanuts, finely chopped
    1 cup almond flour*
    1 teaspoon salt
    ½ teaspoon white pepper
    1 pound fresh okra, cut into ¼-inch pieces
    macadamia nut oil—enough for frying
    * Almond flour is available in most health food stores or organic grocery stores. If you can't find it, it's easy to make. In a food processor, puree roasted almonds until very smooth. That's almond flour. For this recipe, you'll need 6 ounces of almonds.

Stir together the nuts, almond flour, salt, and pepper in a large mixing bowl. Add the okra, and toss until it is well coated. Pour the oil to a depth of 2 inches into a large cast-iron skillet or a Dutch oven. Heat the oil to 375 degrees F. Fry the okra in batches, 4 minutes per batch, and drain on paper towels.

Whole Grains Pilaf

Yield: 6 servings   *Carbohydrates per serving: 15*

Using whole grains is as easy as making any other type of grain, like rice. They just have to cook a little longer.

> ½ cup barley, rinsed
> 3 tablespoons teff
> ¼ cup millet
> kosher salt
> ¾ cup whole wheat farina

In a large saucepan, heat 1½ cups water and bring to a boil. Sprinkle in the barley, stir, and cover. Reduce the heat to low, and cook for 15 minutes. Add the teff, stir, cover, and cook until the water has evaporated, about 25 minutes. In a large skillet or wok over medium-high heat, add millet and toast for about 3 minutes, stirring frequently so as not to burn. Add 1 cup cold water and salt, stir, and cover. Reduce the heat to low, and cook covered for about 15 to 20 minutes until the water evaporates. Remove from heat, fluff with a fork, and cover. Bring 4 cups of water to a boil in a small pot. Add hot water to the barley, increase the heat to medium, and sprinkle in the farina and more salt, whisking to prevent lumps. Simmer until thickened, whisking constantly, about 2 minutes. Add the hot millet to the pilaf, and stir to combine the grains. Divide onto 6 plates, and serve with the cardamom cream.

Cardamom Cream

> 1 cup heavy cream
> 4 cardamom pods, crushed
> 1 tablespoon sesame seeds, toasted

In a small saucepan, heat the cream and the cardamom, and simmer over low heat. Pour this over the pilaf. Sprinkle with toasted sesame seeds.

Cold Cauliflower Salad

Yield: 4 servings   *Carbohydrates per serving: 3*

2 cups cauliflower, chopped into florets
1 tablespoon fresh chopped parsley
1 tablespoon fresh chopped tarragon
1 tablespoon fresh chopped cilantro
1 tablespoon fresh chopped basil
kosher salt
fresh coarse ground black pepper
4 tablespoons macadamia nut oil

In a large stockpot, bring water to a boil and add the cauliflower. Boil for 6 minutes or just until crisp-tender. Drain and submerge in an ice bath for 3 minutes. Drain again, and remove to a large ceramic bowl. Mix in the remaining ingredients, and toss gently to cover all the florets. Season to taste, and refrigerate until ready to use.

Brussels Sprouts Amandine

Yield: 4 servings   *Carbohydrates per serving: 4*

2 tablespoons macadamia nut oil
1 clove garlic, minced
1 teaspoon ground coriander
1 teaspoon cumin
2 cups brussels sprouts, trimmed

In a large skillet, heat the oil. Add the garlic, spices, and the brussels sprouts, and cook over high heat until cooked through, about 10 minutes.

Sauce Amandine

1 tablespoon macadamia nut oil
3 tablespoons sliced almonds
3 tablespoons white wine

Remove the brussels sprouts, and heat another tablespoon of oil over medium-high heat, then add the almonds, and sauté until golden brown. Add the white wine and heat briefly, stirring to combine the flavors. Return the brussels sprouts to the skillet, cook for another 5 minutes, and serve.

Please note that Sauce Amandine can be used for many other vegetables and can even be poured over your favorite grilled or sautéed fish.

Broccoli with Hollandaise Sauce

Yield: 6 servings   *Carbohydrates per serving: 6*

The Hamptons would not be the Hamptons without a few of the old Yankee classics.

1 head broccoli, chopped into florets
½ cup (1 stick) butter
1½ tablespoons freshly squeezed lemon juice
3 egg yolks
1 tablespoon boiling water
3 tablespoons water
¼ teaspoon salt

Steam broccoli florets until crisp-tender. Melt the butter slowly in a small saucepan, and keep warm. Barely heat the lemon juice, and set aside. In the top of a double boiler, over hot but not boiling water, beat 3 egg yolks with a wire whisk until they begin to thicken. Add the boiling water, 1 tablespoon at a time, whisking after each one. Then beat in the lemon juice, continuing to beat while slowly adding the warm butter. Next add the salt, and beat until the sauce is to your desired thickness. Pour over broccoli florets on individual plates.

Thai-Style Stir-Fried Vegetables

Yield: 4 servings   *Carbohydrates per serving: 4*

1 tablespoon sesame seeds
2 tablespoons macadamia nut oil
1 scallion, diced
3 ribs celery, trimmed and peeled, cut into diagonal slices
2 fenugreek leaves
2 small green zucchini, chopped
2 small yellow zucchini, chopped
1 garlic clove, minced
1 teaspoon grated fresh ginger
1 teaspoon lite soy sauce

In a large sauté pan, heat the sesame seeds until they begin to pop. Then add the oil, scallion, celery, and fenugreek, and sauté for 5 minutes. Add the remaining ingredients; pan sauté over high heat until all vegetables are crisp-tender, about 7 to 10 more minutes; and serve.

Lemon Spinach

Yield: 4 servings   *Carbohydrates per serving: 4*

This is another of my mother's hand-me-down, very simple, Southern Italian recipes with a twist.

   4 tablespoons macadamia nut oil
   4 cloves garlic, minced
   1 pound fresh spinach, rinsed and cleaned thoroughly
   salt
   pepper
   1 tablespoon fresh-squeezed lemon juice

In a large skillet, heat the oil over medium-high heat, add the garlic, and sauté for 5 minutes. Add the spinach, and cook, covered, for about 7 minutes, stirring occasionally. Season with salt and pepper, and add the lemon juice.

Gardiner's Zucchini Salad

Yield: 6 servings   *Carbohydrates per serving: 6*

This recipe requires advance preparation.

   2 pounds zucchini, mix of yellow and green
   ½ red onion, thinly sliced
   1 (4-ounce) can mild green chiles, drained and diced
   4 ounces your favorite olives, sliced
   oil and vinegar dressing
   1 avocado, chopped
   ½ cup queso fresco

Cut the zucchini crosswise into ½-inch slices. Cover with water in a saucepan and bring to a boil, reduce heat, and cook about 4 minutes or until just barely tender. Drain, and refresh in cold water. Do not overcook. Drain again. In a stainless steel bowl, combine the zucchini, onion, chilies, and olives; mix with oil and vinegar dressing, and chill at least 2 hours. Before serving, mix in the avocado, and top with the crumbled cheese.

Stone-Ground Corn Fritters

Yield: 6 servings   *Carbohydrates per serving: 14*

½ pound stone-ground corn
½ pound broccoli, very coarsely chopped
½ small onion, finely minced
2 eggs
2 ounces parmesan cheese, freshly grated
macadamia nut oil—enough for frying

Combine all the ingredients except the oil in a large mixing bowl, and blend together until well combined. Heat about ¼ inch of oil on medium-high heat in a large heavy-duty skillet until very hot. Drop the batter by the tablespoon into the hot oil until the batter has been completely used or you run out of room in your skillet. Cook until browned on both sides, about 5 minutes each.

Macadamiaotash

Yield: 8 servings   *Carbohydrates per serving: 20*

In a saucepan, heat 4 tablespoons of macadamia nut oil, and stir in

2 cups cooked corn kernels
1½ cups cooked lima beans or
1¾ cup cut green beans
¼ cup finely chopped green onion, including part of the top
½ cup whipping cream
salt
pepper

Simmer until slightly thickened and heated through. Salt and pepper to taste.

Three Mile Asparagus

Yield: 10 servings   *Carbohydrates per serving: 4*

Please note that this recipe requires a long preparation time so it is best made the night before you wish to serve it.

½ cup fresh lemon juice
6 tablespoons macadamia nut oil
¼ teaspoon salt
¼ teaspoon pepper
1 garlic clove, minced
1 (14-ounce) can artichoke heart quarters, drained
4 ounces diced pimientos
2 pounds fresh asparagus, peeled and trimmed

Whisk together the lemon juice and the next four ingredients in a large stainless steel bowl. Add the artichoke hearts and the pimientos, and gently toss. Cover, and chill at least 8 hours or overnight. Cook the asparagus in boiling salted water until crisp-tender, about 3 minutes. Drain the asparagus, and plunge into ice water to stop the cooking process. Place cooked asparagus in a large heavy-duty resealable plastic bag, and store overnight in the refrigerator, if desired. After the artichokes have marinated, add the asparagus to the artichoke mixture, and gently toss. Cover, and chill for another 2 hours. Please note that this part of the recipe should be followed exactly. Do not marinate asparagus in the mixture containing lemon juice for more than 2 hours, as the juice can discolor and toughen the asparagus.

Green Beans with Lemon

Yield: 4 servings   *Carbohydrates per serving: 3*

1 teaspoon salt
1 pound of tiny green beans
4 tablespoons macadamia nut oil
2 tablespoons grated lemon rind
1 tablespoon fresh lemon juice
1 teaspoon pepper

Bring 2 quarts of water to a boil in a heavy saucepan. Add the salt and green beans. Cook about 7 minutes, then plunge into ice water to stop the cooking process; drain. Heat the oil in a heavy saucepan over medium heat; add the beans, and sauté for 2 minutes. Add lemon rind, and sauté an additional minute. Stir in lemon juice and pepper. Serve immediately.

Brown Rice and Chicken Salad

Yield: 4 servings   *Carbohydrates per serving: 18*

- 2 cups water
- 1 pound chicken breast, cubed
- 1 teaspoon celery seed
- ½ cup uncooked brown rice
- salt
- pepper

Bring the water to a boil in a medium stockpot. Add the chicken, and cook until tender, about 15 minutes. Remove the chicken, and skim any fat out of the pot. While the water is boiling, add the celery seed and the rice; reduce the heat to a simmer, and cover for 30 minutes. Remove from heat, season with salt and pepper to taste, and fluff with a fork. Gently mix the chicken through the rice, and serve.

Etruscan Spinach

Yield: 4 servings   *Carbohydrates per serving: 4*

- 1 pound baby spinach
- 2 tablespoons macadamia nut oil
- 2 garlic cloves, minced
- ¼ teaspoon salt
- ¼ teaspoon pepper
- 2 tablespoons pine nuts, toasted

Clean the spinach thoroughly. In a large skillet, heat the oil over medium-high heat until it is shimmering, place the spinach and garlic in the skillet, and sauté for about 5 minutes or until the spinach starts to wilt. Stir in the salt and pepper; sprinkle with pine nuts, and serve immediately.

Oven-Baked Mushroom Polenta

Yield: 6 servings   *Carbohydrates per serving: 14*

2 quarts organic chicken stock
2 tablespoons macadamia nut oil
kosher salt
1 portobello mushroom, finely chopped
12 ounces whole-grain polenta meal, not instant
macadamia nut oil spray

In a large saucepan, bring the stock to a boil, and then immediately reduce to a simmer. While waiting for the pot to boil, in a small skillet heat the oil and sauté the mushroom until tender, about 3 minutes. Remove from heat, and drain. Slowly pour the polenta into the stock, stirring rapidly with a wooden spoon. Reduce to medium heat and slowly bring to a boil, stirring constantly. Add salt to taste. Boil for 5 more minutes, then pour the polenta into a 3-quart shallow baking dish that has been sprayed with oil. Gently fold in the mushroom. Cover with buttered foil, and bake for 1 hour in a 350-degree F preheated oven. Remove the foil, and serve.

Neapolitan Cauliflower

Yield: 6 servings   *Carbohydrates per serving: 6*

1 large head cauliflower, cut into florets
kosher salt
freshly ground coarse black pepper
2 cups macadamia nut oil
grated zest of 2 lemons
3 cloves garlic, peeled
2 tablespoons fresh thyme leaves, chopped
ground red pepper
2 tablespoons capers, rinsed well
¼ cup pitted kalamata olives, chopped fine
juice of one lime, freshly squeezed

Place the cauliflower in a large bowl, and season with the salt and black pepper. Pour about ⅓ cup oil over the cauliflower and mix well, making sure to coat all the florets. Spread out on a baking sheet, and roast in a 375-degree F preheated oven for 30 minutes. Remove from the oven, and allow to cool. In a small saucepan, combine the lemon zest, garlic, thyme, red pepper, and 1 cup of oil. Heat until just boiling, and cook for about 20 minutes or until the garlic is soft. Allow to cool and puree in a blender or a food processor. In another saucepan, combine the capers, olives, and ½ cup oil, and warm this for about 5 minutes. Transfer the cauliflower to a serving bowl, pour ½ the garlic-lemon oil into the bowl, and toss to coat. Spoon in the caper-olive mixture, and toss again. Just before serving, sprinkle with fresh lime juice.

Dressy Springs Salad

Yield: 4 servings   *Carbohydrates per serving: 5*

> 1 large head iceberg lettuce, cut into 4 wedges
> Blue Cheese Dressing (see recipe below)
> 6 bacon slices, cooked and crumbled
> ½ cup shredded parmesan cheese
> ¼ cup chopped fresh chives

Place a lettuce wedge on each plate. Pour the dressing over the lettuce. Combine the bacon, cheese, and chives in a small bowl, then sprinkle over the dressing. Naturally, any dressing can be used in this recipe. The iceberg wedge with blue cheese is a classic steakhouse tradition. The Hamptons are very big on old traditions, and you get a good dose of monounsaturates in this recipe.

Blue Cheese Dressing

> 1 cup Maconnaise (see recipe on page 205)
> 1 (8-ounce) container sour cream
> 4 ounces crumbled blue cheese
> ¼ teaspoon salt
> 1 teaspoon lemon juice

Stir together all the ingredients in a small bowl, and chill until ready to serve. This, like all salad dressings, can be made in advance, so double this recipe and save it for a few days.

North Haven Lentil Salad

Yield: 4 servings   *Carbohydrates per serving: 12*

This recipe requires preparation time.

 ¼ cup macadamia nut oil
 ⅛ cup white wine vinegar
 ¼ teaspoon fines herbes
 2 tablespoons fresh lemon juice
 ½ teaspoon ground cumin
 ½ teaspoon salt
 ½ teaspoon fresh ground black pepper
 ¼ teaspoon crushed red pepper
 2 cups cooked lentils
 ½ red bell pepper, diced fine
 ½ small onions, diced fine
 1½ tablespoons chopped fresh cilantro

Whisk together the first eight ingredients in a medium-sized stainless steel bowl. Add the lentils and the remaining ingredients, tossing gently to coat. Cover, and chill for at least 2 hours.

Please note that this recipe can also be used as a side salad and can actually serve 8, which would bring the total carbohydrate count per serving down to 4.5.

Southern Sophisticate Corn Pilaf

Yield: 6 servings   *Carbohydrates per serving: 15*

This is basically made the same way as the Whole Grains Pilaf but with different grains. I included other grains so that you could see how easy they are to cook.

 ½ cup kamut, rinsed
 salt
 ¾ cup yellow stone-ground corn grits, not instant
 ¼ cup amaranth
 ¼ cup quinoa, rinsed
 2 tablespoons macadamia nut oil
 2 tablespoons flaxseed oil
 3 tablespoons flaxseeds, toasted

In a skillet or a wok, heat the kamut and toss frequently until grains begin to pop, about 3 minutes. Add 1 cup of water and some salt (to taste), reduce heat, stir, and cover. Cook until the water has evaporated, about 25 minutes; remove from heat, stir, and cover. In a large saucepan, bring 5 cups of water to a boil; sprinkle in grits and salt, reduce the heat to low, and allow to cook for 10 minutes, stirring frequently. Sprinkle in the amaranth and quinoa, and stir to combine. Continue to simmer, stirring frequently, until the grains are tender, about 15 minutes. Add the hot kamut and macadamia nut oil to the pilaf, and stir to combine. Remove to plates, and sprinkle with flaxseed oil and toasted flaxseeds.

Nutty Asparagus

Yield: 8 servings   *Carbohydrates per serving: 4*

  2 pounds fresh asparagus, peeled and trimmed
  2 tablespoons macadamia nut oil
  1 tablespoon lime juice
  ¾ cup slivered almonds, toasted
  salt, to taste
  pepper, to taste

Cook the asparagus in boiling salted water for 3 to 5 minutes or just until crisp-tender; drain, then plunge into an ice bath, and drain again. In a large skillet, heat the oil over medium heat; add the asparagus, and sauté for 3 to 5 minutes. Toss the asparagus with the lime juice and almonds. Season with salt and pepper to taste.

Chinese Cabbage Coleslaw

Yield: 10 servings   *Carbohydrates per serving: 2*

The reason I chose Chinese cabbage is that it has fewer carbohydrates than traditional red or green cabbage does.

  1 (8-ounce) container sour cream
  2 tablespoons white wine vinegar
  2 teaspoons celery seeds
  1 teaspoon salt
  ¼ teaspoon ground cumin
  16 ounces finely shredded Chinese cabbage

Stir together all the ingredients except the cabbage in a large bowl. Mix well. Add the shredded cabbage, tossing to coat. Chill until ready to serve.

Southwestern Variation

To make this more southwestern in flair, simply add ½ teaspoon of ground chipotle pepper, ½ teaspoon of chili pepper, and 1 tablespoon of Tabasco, and prepare in the same way as the previous recipe.

Rose Hill Collard Greens

Yield: 8 servings   *Carbohydrates per serving: 4.*
This will depend on the chosen vegetable.

This recipe is a basic stir fry and can be used to stir fry any vegetable that I included in the menu section. The only difference is the amount of time necessary to cook the vegetables.

    ¾ teaspoon salt
    2 pounds collard greens
    1 small onion, finely diced
    6 cloves garlic, chopped
    ¼ teaspoon crushed red pepper
    1 teaspoon mustard seeds
    ½ teaspoon ground cumin
    2 tablespoons macadamia nut oil

Bring a pot of salted water to a boil, and blanch the collards in the boiling water for about 1 minute. Put immediately into an ice bath to stop the cooking, and drain well. Sauté the onion, garlic, red pepper, mustard seeds, and cumin in the oil over high heat for about 5 minutes or until the onion is tender. Add greens and a dash of salt, and stir constantly for about 3 minutes. Taste, adjust the seasonings, and serve.

Stuffed Zucchini Sedona Style

Yield: 6 servings   *Carbohydrates per serving: 4*

   6 medium zucchini
   ¾ teaspoon salt
   3 ounces of Monterey Jack cheese, shredded
   ½ cup chopped green onions
   6 bacon slices, cooked and crumbled
   3 small tomatillos, husked and chopped fine
   ½ teaspoon pepper
   ½ cup parmesan cheese
   2 tablespoons chilled butter

Cut zucchini in half lengthwise, and remove the seeds. Parboil the zucchini until just tender for about 3 minutes in boiling salted water. Scoop out the pulp, keeping the shells intact. This can also be done in a microwave oven, although I don't recommend using one. If you like, place the zucchini in an 11- × 7-inch glass dish, and microwave on high for 5 to 7 minutes or until just tender. Reserve the pulp, and sprinkle the shells with salt. Stir together in a small mixing bowl the pulp, the Monterey Jack cheese, and the next four ingredients. Fill the shells with the pulp mixture, and place in a 13- × 9-inch baking dish. Sprinkle evenly with the parmesan, and cut the butter over the parmesan. Bake uncovered in a preheated 375-degree F oven for 30 minutes.

Mediterranean Couscous Salad

Yield: 8 servings   *Carbohydrates per serving: 25*

¾ cup vegetable broth
1 cup uncooked couscous
4 tablespoons macadamia nut oil
1 (14-ounce) can artichoke hearts, drained and coarsely chopped
10 ounces green chilies, finely diced
½ cup crumbled feta cheese
¼ cup pine nuts, toasted
¼ cup pitted kalamata olives
2 green onions, chopped
1 garlic clove, minced
2 tablespoons chopped fresh basil
2 tablespoons chopped fresh mint
2 tablespoons chopped fresh parsley

Bring the broth to a boil in a heavy saucepan, then stir in the cous-cous. Cover, return to a boil and remove from heat. Let stand for 5 minutes. Drizzle in the oil, fluff with a fork, and let cool. Combine the couscous, the artichokes, and the next nine ingredients, tossing gently. Serve.

Warm Coleslaw Salad

Yield: 10 servings   *Carbohydrates per serving: 8*

½ pound finely diced salt pork
3 tablespoons white wine vinegar
2 tablespoons water
1 teaspoon celery seed (caraway would work, too)
1 teaspoon salt
3 cups shredded cabbage
2 ounces macadamia nuts, chopped into small pieces

Place the salt pork in a large heavy skillet, and render the fat slowly. Remove the crisp brown pieces, drain on paper towels, and reserve. To the rendered fat in the skillet, add all other ingredients except the nuts and cabbage. Cook over high heat until it boils. Reduce heat to a simmer, and stir in the cabbage. Simmer for 1 minute longer, and serve garnished with the reserved cubes of salt pork and the macadamia nuts.

West Hampton Eggplant Vinaigrette

Yield: 6 servings   *Carbohydrates per serving: 6*

This recipe requires some advance preparation time.

    2 large eggplants
    2½ teaspoons salt
    2 small zucchini
    2 yellow squash
    8 tablespoons macadamia nut oil
    4 garlic cloves, minced
    ¼ cup chopped fresh basil
    ¼ cup chopped fresh thyme
    ¼ cup chopped fresh Italian parsley
    3 tablespoons red wine vinegar
    macadamia nut oil spray

Cut eggplants crosswise into ½-inch slices, and sprinkle the sides with 1½ teaspoons of the salt. Place the slices in a single layer on paper towels, and let stand for 1 hour. In the meantime, cut the zucchini and squash lengthwise into ¼-inch thick slices or thinner, and set aside. In a food processor, put ½ teaspoon salt, macadamia nut oil, minced garlic, basil, thyme, parsley, and vinegar, and process this, stopping occasionally to scrape down the sides. Rinse the eggplant with water, and pat dry. Brush the slices with the oil mixture, and sprinkle with another ¼ teaspoon salt. Arrange the eggplant in a single layer on a lightly oil-sprayed grill. Grill the eggplant slices, covered, on medium-high heat for 10 to 12 minutes or until lightly browned, turning and brushing with the oil mixture. When done, remove from grill. Sprinkle the zucchini and squash slices with ¼ teaspoon salt, brush with the oil mixture, and grill them in the same manner as the eggplant but for only about 5 minutes on one side and 2 minutes on the other. Arrange the grilled vegetables in an even layer in a 13- × 9-inch baking dish. Pour the remaining oil mixture over the vegetables, cover, and chill for 8 hours.

Steakhouse Wedge Salad

Yield: 4 servings   *Carbohydrates per serving: 2*

    4 bacon slices
    1 medium onion, sliced thin
    2 cups heavy cream
    ½ cup sour cream
    coarse ground black pepper
    ½ teaspoon red chili pepper
    ¼ cup chopped fresh basil
    2 garlic cloves
    1 large head iceberg lettuce, cut into 4 wedges

Cook the bacon in a large skillet until crisp, remove, drain on paper towels, and crumble; reserve 1 tablespoon of drippings in the skillet. Sauté the onion in the hot drippings over medium heat for 10 minutes or until tender and lightly browned. Remove from heat, and allow to cool. In a food processor, combine the heavy cream, sour cream, black pepper, red chili pepper, basil, and garlic, and process until smooth and creamy. Top each lettuce wedge with the dressing, cooked onion, and bacon.

Smothered Belle Green Beans

Yield: 6 servings   *Carbohydrates per serving: 5*

    4 tablespoons macadamia nut oil
    3 celery ribs, peeled and chopped
    1 pound fresh green beans, trimmed
    1 medium onion, chopped
    1 red bell pepper, chopped
    1 orange bell pepper, chopped
    2 garlic cloves, minced
    1 sprig fresh thyme, chopped
    ½ cup fresh basil, chopped
    ¼ teaspoon black pepper
    ½ teaspoon salt
    4 bacon slices, cooked and crumbled

Heat 4 tablespoons of oil in a large skillet. Cook the celery, green beans, onions, and both peppers over medium-high heat until tender, about 12 to 15 minutes. Add the next five ingredients and continue to cook, stirring often, for about 5 minutes more or until the beans are tender. Stir in the bacon.

Grilled Zucchini

Yield: 4 servings   *Carbohydrates per serving: 1*

> 5 medium zucchini
> ¼ cup macadamia nut oil
> salt
> juice of 1 lemon, fresh-squeezed

Trim the ends of the zucchini, and slice each lengthwise. In a large shallow dish, combine the oil and the zucchini slices, coating well. Use a large griddle over medium-high heat, and when it's hot, place the zucchini slices in a single layer on the griddle, turning frequently to get the scorch marks placed perfectly. When ready to serve, sprinkle the zucchini with salt and lemon juice. This can be served hot or at room temperature.

Sweet Potato Gratin

Yield: 8 servings   *Carbohydrates per serving: 18*

This recipe is adapted from Tom Valenti's outrageously delicious potato gratin recipe, found in his book *Welcome to My Kitchen,* published by HarperCollins in 2002. I just made it a little more healthful by switching the potato to a sweet potato.

> 1 pint heavy whipping cream
> 4 sprigs fresh thyme
> 2 bay leaves
> 15 black peppercorns
> 15 cloves garlic, smashed
> unsalted butter for baking dish
> 4 medium sweet potatoes, cut into ⅛ inch slices using a mandoline
> salt
> fresh ground black pepper

Place the cream in a saucepan over high heat. Add the thyme, bay leaves, peppercorns, and 12 cloves of the garlic. Bring to a boil, and immediately lower to a simmer. Simmer for 15 to 20 minutes, until the cream takes on all the flavors. In the final few minutes of the cooking process, add the remaining 3 cloves of garlic. Strain the cream, and discard the solids.

Lightly butter a 12-inch round baking dish, and cover the surface with a layer of potato slices. Dust with salt and pepper, and spoon some of the cream mixture over the top. Repeat with another layer of potatoes, seasoning, and cream until the gratin reaches a height of 2 inches. Press down gently on the potatoes to bring the cream to the top. Cover with aluminum foil and place in a preheated oven at 375 degrees F. Bake for 35 to 40 minutes, remove the foil, and continue to cook until the top is browned or the gratin is done (when a thin knife slips easily into the center).

Jalapeno Babies

Yield: 6 servings   *Carbohydrates per serving: 2*

This recipe is an addition to the vegetable section, as it is not included in the 30-day meal plan. It can be used as a side vegetable or, if you double the ingredients and slice the peppers in half, as an appetizer on a sizzling hot August night.

> 6 large fresh jalapeno peppers
> 4 ounces cream cheese
> 4 slices bacon, uncooked

Core the jalapenos, and remove the seeds—you should probably wear plastic gloves for this step of the procedure. Stuff each jalapeno with cream cheese, wrap in bacon, and secure with a wet toothpick. Bake in a preheated 375-degree F oven for 20 to 25 minutes until the bacon is crisp. Serve hot from the oven. If served as an appetizer, simply slice the peppers lengthwise in half.

Roasted Asparagus with Shallots

Yield: 8 servings   *Carbohydrates per serving: 4*

2 pounds fresh asparagus, peeled and trimmed
¼ cup macadamia nut oil, divided
1 shallot, minced
2 tablespoons white wine vinegar
salt, to taste
pepper, to taste

Toss asparagus with 2 tablespoons of the oil, and place in a large baking dish. Bake in a preheated 400-degree F oven for 40 to 45 minutes, stirring occasionally. Stir together the shallot and the vinegar, and season with salt and pepper to taste. Gradually mix in the remaining oil. Pour over the asparagus.

Quinoa Amontillado

Yield: 6 servings   *Carbohydrates per serving: 25*

This is another recipe adapted from one created by Doug Rodriguez.

½ pound quinoa
3 cloves garlic, minced
¼ cup macadamia nut oil
1 small red bell pepper, seeded, de-ribbed, and finely diced
½ cup finely chopped fresh flat-leaf parsley
½ cup kalamata olives, pitted and diced small
Salt

Rinse the quinoa in a bowl of cold water, and rub between your fingers; repeat until the water is clear. Place the quinoa and enough water to cover in a medium saucepan, and bring to a boil over high heat. Lower heat, and simmer for 10 minutes or until the quinoa is translucent. Drain, and run under cold water to rinse. Drain again, and set aside. In a small saucepan over high heat, sauté the garlic in the oil for 1 minute; add the bell pepper, and continue to sauté for another 2 minutes, until soft. Blend the sautéed mixture and the remaining ingredients into the quinoa, and serve at room temperature.

Bayou-Fresh Vegetables

Yield: 8 servings   *Carbohydrates per serving: 6*

The beauty of this dish is that you can use whatever is fresh at the vegetable stand that day. This recipe is all about the dressing. It takes a bit of advance preparation time.

3 tablespoons macadamia nut oil
1 pound fresh broccoli, trimmed and cut into florets
8 ounces fresh mushrooms—your favorite—chopped
1 orange bell pepper sliced
1 yellow bell pepper sliced
3 medium zucchini sliced
½ purple onion
Bayou Dressing (recipe follows)

Cook the broccoli in boiling salted water for about 5 minutes; drain, plunge into ice water to stop the cooking process, and drain again. In a large skillet, heat the oil and add the mushrooms, peppers, and zucchini, using high heat for 3 minutes, just until vegetables are lightly cooked. Remove from heat, and drain. Combine the broccoli with the mushroom/vegetable mixture in a large bowl, add the onion, and toss with Bayou Dressing. Cover, and chill for at least 2 hours.

Bayou Dressing

Yield: ¾ cup

2 tablespoons mustard
⅓ cup macadamia nut oil
⅓ cup red wine vinegar
¼ teaspoon salt
½ teaspoon ground chili pepper
½ teaspoon ground garlic
½ teaspoon Tabasco

Whisk together all ingredients in a small bowl, and blend well.

Hamptons Bay Beans

Yield: 4 servings   *Carbohydrates per serving: 4*

¾ teaspoon salt
1 pound fresh green beans, trimmed
4 tablespoons macadamia nut oil
1 small onion, minced
1 celery rib, peeled and cut on the diagonal
2 garlic cloves, minced
2 sprigs fresh rosemary, chopped
¼ cup chopped fresh Italian parsley

Bring salted water to a boil in a large saucepan. Add the beans, cover, and cook for 10 to 12 minutes or just until tender. Drain, and plunge into an ice bath to stop the cooking process; drain again. In a saucepan, heat the oil over medium-high heat; when heated, add the onion and celery, and sauté for 5 minutes. Add the garlic, and sauté for 2 additional minutes. Stir in the beans, rosemary, salt to taste, and parsley; sauté for 5 minutes or until well heated through.

Chilled Laotian Asparagus

Yield: 4 servings   *Carbohydrates per serving: 3*

This takes some preparation time.

¾ cup rice vinegar
1½ tablespoons fresh ginger, minced
1 pound fresh asparagus, trimmed and peeled
½ teaspoon salt
1 garlic clove, minced
6 tablespoons macadamia nut oil
1 teaspoon lite soy sauce

Bring vinegar and ginger to a boil in a small saucepan, and boil until half the liquid has been reduced. Remove from heat, and set aside. Place the asparagus in boiling salted water for 5 minutes or just until crisp-tender. Drain. Plunge into an ice bath to stop the cooking, and drain again. Arrange the asparagus spears on a serving platter. In a small bowl stir together the garlic, oil, soy sauce, and salt to taste, then mix well. Drizzle over the asparagus, cover, and chill for 30 minutes. Drizzle the vinegar mixture over the asparagus, and chill again for 1 hour.

Desserts

Georgica Cheesecake

Yield: 12 servings   *Carbohydrates per serving: 8*

1½ cups shredded, unsweetened coconut for the crust and another ½ cup
     for the cheesecake
1 cup sugar substitute, divided
1 cup (2 sticks) melted unsalted butter
32 ounces cream cheese, softened
3 eggs
1 egg yolk
1 (11-ounce) can of unsweetened coconut milk
1 cup heavy whipping cream

Combine 1½ cups of shredded coconut, ¼ cup sugar substitute, and
butter in a medium bowl, and mix thoroughly. Press over the bottom
and up the side of a buttered 9-inch springform pan. Chill in the refrigerator. Beat the cream cheese and ¾ cup sugar substitute in a large
bowl until smooth and fluffy. Add the eggs and egg yolk, one at a time,
beating well after each addition. Beat in the coconut milk, 1 cup heavy
cream, ½ cup shredded coconut just until blended. Pour into the prepared pan. In a preheated 300-degree F oven, bake for 1½ hours or
until puffed and golden brown. Cool on a wire rack and chill, covered,
in the refrigerator.

Variation

Simply puree your favorite berries in a small food processor or
blender, and pour over the cheesecake.

Ricotta Dessert Flan

Yield: 6 servings   *Carbohydrates per serving: 2*

1 cup ricotta
2 large eggs
½ cup farmer's cheese
½ teaspoon salt
2 packets Stevia
½ teaspoon vanilla extract
macadamia nut oil spray

In a medium bowl, combine the ricotta and eggs, and mix until smooth. Add the farmer's cheese, salt, Stevia, and vanilla, and mix again until smooth. Pour the batter into small ramekins that have been sprayed with macadamia nut oil. Bake in a preheated 350-degree F oven for only 12 to 15 minutes. Allow to cool for 5 minutes and then remove, turning upside down onto plate.

Coconut Cream Pie

Yield: 4 servings   *Carbohydrates per serving: 4*

1 pound queso blanco, divided into 4 even pieces
8 ounces shredded, unsweetened coconut
8 ounces heavy cream
4 tablespoons sour cream
4 macadamia nuts

Put each slice of queso blanco onto an oven-ready dessert plate. Sprinkle with coconut, and place in a preheated 400-degree F oven for about 5 minutes or until the cheese starts to melt. Remove from heat, and allow to cool for 5 minutes. Pour the cream over each one; dollop with the sour cream and place one nut on top of each dollop of sour cream.

Raspberry Cheesecake Squares

Yield: 8 servings   *Carbohydrates per serving: 2*

This recipe is a big favorite of my patients. You can use any diet-flavored gelatin you like, so that you always have a different dessert.

    1 package sugar-free raspberry gelatin
    1 cup boiling water
    2 (8-ounce) packages cream cheese, softened

Sprinkle the gelatin into the boiling water, and stir until well dissolved. In a bowl, beat the cream cheese until it is very creamy. With the mixer running, add the gelatin, ¼ cup at a time, and mix until thoroughly combined. Pour into an 8- × 8-inch pan, and refrigerate until firm, about 2 hours.

Mixed Berry Float

Yield: 2 servings   *Carbohydrates per serving: 6*

    8 ounces heavy whipping cream
    1 ounce berries and 1 ounce reserved
    ice
    8 ounces water

Combine all the ingredients except the reserved berries in a blender, and liquefy. Pour into two parfait glasses, and top with the reserved berries.

Coconut Macadamiaroons

Yield: 16 servings   *Carbohydrates per serving: 10 (2 cookies)*

    8 ounces unsweetened shredded coconut
    8 ounces almond flour (any nut flour can be used)
    4 tablespoons macadamia nut oil
    1 tablespoon sugar substitute

Combine all ingredients in a stainless steel bowl until well mixed. For each cookie, spoon a tablespoonful of the mixture onto a cookie sheet. Bake in a preheated 325-degree F oven for about 6 minutes or until the cookies just start to get browned. Remove from heat, and allow to cool on a wire rack.

Blackberry Float

Yield: 1 serving   *Carbohydrates per serving: 6*

This can be made with the berry of your choosing, as a variation.

½ cup blackberries
½ cup heavy whipping cream
ice

Combine all the ingredients in a blender, and liquefy until the ice is crunchy. This can even be made in a larger quantity. Add 1 cup of water, pour into Popsicle molds, and freeze. It's great for the kids.

Coconut Cream Pie Ice

Yield: 4 servings   *Carbohydrates per serving: 6*

This basic recipe can be made into a variation for any berry or any fruit flavoring that you prefer. The carbohydrate count per serving may vary slightly, depending on which fruit you choose.

1 cup heavy whipping cream
1 cup unsweetened, shredded coconut
ice

Combine all the ingredients in a blender until well liquefied. Pour into parfait cups, and freeze.

Variation

Lemon Cream Ice: Use the same recipe, and add juice from 1 lemon or 1 lime. Please note that this recipe may require a teaspoon of artificial sweetener.

Dressings, Dips, and Salads

Oil and Vinegar Dressing

Yield: about ½ cup   *Carbohydrates per serving: 0*

    1 clove garlic, crushed
    2 tablespoons white wine vinegar
    salt
    pepper
    ½ cup macadamia nut oil

Combine all ingredients into a shaker or a bowl, and mix until blended well.

Traditional Caesar Dressing

Yield: ½ cup   *Carbohydrates per serving: 1*

    4 anchovy fillets, mashed (optional)
    ½ teaspoon Dijon mustard
    2 cloves garlic, minced
    2 tablespoons fresh-squeezed lemon juice
    1 egg yolk (if you're afraid of raw egg, simply substitute 1 tablespoon of
        Maconnaise)
    ½ cup macadamia nut oil
    ½ cup freshly grated parmesan cheese
    kosher salt
    freshly ground coarse black pepper

In a small bowl, whisk together all the ingredients until well combined. Season to taste. Pour over the salad, traditionally romaine, but whichever greens are fresh from the farm that day will suffice.

Arugula and Shaved Parmesan Salad

Carbohydrates per serving: 2

This is a variation on a green salad, except you use arugula as your lettuce leaves. Arugula, when picked fresh, has a deliciously bitter and pungent taste that holds up well to a nice aged parmesan. Simply prepare the arugula as you would any other lettuce, choose your dressing, toss with the greens, and put on a plate. Then, shave some of your best parmesan over the salad. One to two very thin slices will be delicious.

Nutty Parmesan Salad

Carbohydrates per serving: 4

This is the same as a regular salad with your favorite dressing and shaved parmesan added, as described previously. The only other difference is that you may add 2 ounces of your favorite nut (pecans, walnuts, and macadamia nuts work well here), toasted, to the salad to give it more texture.

Chopped Salad

Yield: 4 servings   *Carbohydrates per serving: 4*

This is a great way to change your typical salad. I really enjoy having my salad prepared this way. Even though the ingredients are the same as those in your regular tossed salad, chopping all the ingredients makes it taste different. It's also best to use seasonal greens in a chopped salad, as they tend to be crisper. Seasonal in the northern hemisphere is spinach, Belgian endive, and baby mustard greens in the winter; and arugula, Bibb, watercress, and many others in the summer.

    8 cups seasonal greens, finely chopped
    1 small red onion, finely chopped
    2 stalks of celery, peeled and finely chopped
    1 cucumber, peeled and finely chopped
    4 ounces stilton cheese
    4 ounces pancetta, cut into a fine dice
    3 tablespoons shallots, diced
    3 tablespoons red wine vinegar
    ⅓ cup macadamia nut oil

The first four ingredients can be chopped in a food processor. In a large bowl, combine the greens, onion, celery, cucumber, and cheese. In a medium skillet over medium-high heat, cook the pancetta until the fat has been rendered. Add the shallots, and cook until the pancetta is crisp and the shallots are translucent, about 6 minutes. Transfer the pancetta and shallots to the bowl with the greens. Add vinegar to the skillet, and cook for 1 minute. Remove from heat, and whisk in the oil. Pour over the greens, and toss well.

Onion Cucumber Salad

Yield: 8 servings   *Carbohydrates per serving: 4*

    2 large onions
    3 cucumbers, halved and seeded, unpeeled
    2 quarts ice cubes
    ¼ cup white wine vinegar
    ½ tablespoon salt

Slice the onions and cucumbers, and layer with ice in a shallow bowl; pour on the vinegar, and add salt.

Greek Salad

                                             Carbohydrates per serving: 4

This is another variation on the tossed lettuce concept. To make an interesting salad requires nothing more than a little imagination and different ingredients.

    ½ teaspoon dried oregano
    1 clove garlic, minced
    6 radishes, sliced thin
    1 cup assorted olives
    6 ounces feta cheese, crumbled (I often get the one with peppercorns,
        which adds flavor and texture to the dish)

Put whichever greens you choose in a bowl. Take your basic oil and vinegar dressing, and combine with the previous ingredients. Pour into a bowl, and toss thoroughly.

Endive and Roquefort Salad

Yield: 4 servings   *Carbohydrates per serving: 4*

This is adapted from one of my all-time favorite salads, created by one of my favorite chefs of all time, Thomas Valenti.

    3 ounces bacon, diced
    4 large Belgian endives
    4 ounces Roquefort cheese, crumbled
    1 cup sherry vinaigrette
    2 tablespoons minced chives
    2 tablespoons minced flat-leaf parsley
    freshly ground black pepper

Cook the bacon in a sauté pan over medium-high heat until well done, about 6 minutes. Cut the endives in half lengthwise, and with the cut side down, slice into thin strips. On each of four plates, arrange the endive into a square plank. Sprinkle the plank with cheese, then drizzle the vinaigrette, chives, and parsley, using about half of each. Season with pepper, and lay another plank perpendicular to the first one on top. Drain the bacon on paper towels, and distribute evenly among the 4 plates. Drizzle with the remaining vinaigrette, chives, and parsley, and serve.

Sherry Vinaigrette

    3 tablespoons Dijon mustard
    1 egg yolk
    4 teaspoons sherry vinegar
    ¾ cup macadamia nut oil
    salt
    pepper

In a mixing bowl, whisk together the mustard and the egg yolk. Whisk in 1 teaspoon of the vinegar, then slowly whisk in the oil to make a thick emulsion. Whisk in the rest of the vinegar, and season with salt and pepper.

Sydneysider Salad

Carbohydrates per serving: 4

This is another variation of a basic salad with your favorite dressing. Simply add 2 ounces of toasted macadamia nuts and 2 ounces of shredded sheep's milk cheese, and you get a salad served everywhere Down Under in Sydney.

Bacon and Roquefort Dressing

Yield: 4 servings   *Carbohydrates per serving: 2*

    2 tablespoons Maconnaise
    2 tablespoons heavy cream
    1 teaspoon Dijon mustard
    1 teaspoon horseradish
    4 ounces Roquefort cheese, crumbled
    4 slices bacon, cooked and crumbled

Mix all ingredients together well.

Creamy Peanut Dressing

Yield: 4 servings   *Carbohydrates per serving: 2*

    2 tablespoons Maconnaise
    2 tablespoons heavy cream
    1 teaspoon Dijon mustard
    1 teaspoon horseradish
    1 tablespoon crunchy, unsweetened peanut butter

Mix all ingredients together in a small food processor until smooth.

Sour Cream Dressing

Yield: 8 servings   *Carbohydrates per serving: 2*

    3 hard-cooked eggs
    juice of 1 lemon, freshly squeezed
    1 cup sour cream
    2 tablespoons heavy cream
    salt
    pepper

Put the egg yolks and the rest of the ingredients in a food processor, and pulse until smooth. You may thin it with extra cream to gain the desired consistency.

Warm Braised Spinach Salad with Pecans

Carbohydrates per serving: 4

Instead of dressing your spinach, first heat it in a medium skillet with a few tablespoons of macadamia nut oil until just heated through, about 2 minutes. Dress it as you normally would, and sprinkle on a tablespoon of toasted pecans.

Many of the following dips can be used as marinades for the meat dishes, so this adds another dimension to your menu planning.

Cheese and Beef Dip

Yield: 12 servings   *Carbohydrates per serving: 2*

  1 pound ground beef—91% lean
  2 green onions, sliced
  fajita seasonings
  ¾ cup water
  1 teaspoon crushed red pepper
  salt
  8 ounces Monterey Jack, shredded

Cook the beef in a skillet until cooked through, about 8 minutes; drain, and return the beef to the skillet. Add all the remaining ingredients except the cheese, bring to a boil, reduce heat, and simmer for 5 minutes. Stir in the cheese until melted, and simmer for another 10 minutes until thickened, stirring constantly. Remove from heat, and place in a dipping bowl.

Horseradish Dip

Yield: 24 servings   *Carbohydrates per serving: 1*

  2 (8-ounce) packages cream cheese
  1 garlic clove, minced
  1 teaspoon fines herbes
  3 tablespoons fresh horseradish
  ¼ cup sour cream
  1 tablespoon chopped fresh dill

Allow the cream cheese to soften, then combine all the ingredients in a bowl and chill.

Cilantro Nut Dip

Yield: 24 servings   *Carbohydrates per serving: 1*

1 cup chopped fresh cilantro
¼ cup fresh grated parmesan cheese
½ cup chopped macadamia nuts
2 cloves garlic, minced
8 ounces smooth goat cheese
¼ cup macadamia nut oil
kosher salt to taste

Combine all the ingredients except the oil in a food processor, and pulse until well combined. Gradually add in the oil, processing until smooth. This can even be used on meats and fish—it is that rich.

Spinach Avocado Dip

Yield: 24 servings   *Carbohydrates per serving: 1*

2 cups fresh spinach leaves
¼ cup heavy cream
½ red onion, finely diced
1 tablespoon green chilies
1 teaspoon fresh-squeezed lime juice
¼ cup fresh chopped cilantro
½ medium avocado, peeled and sliced

Cook the spinach in a pot of boiling salted water for about 1 minute. Drain, and rinse under cold water; drain again, and squeeze dry. Put the remaining ingredients except the avocado in a food processor, and pulse until the spinach is finely chopped, but don't overblend. Mash the avocado separately, then stir into the spinach mixture.

Pesto Dip

Yield: 12 servings   *Carbohydrates per serving: 1*

   ¼ cup fresh pesto
   1 teaspoon lime juice, freshly squeezed
   ½ cup Maconnaise
   ¼ teaspoon salt
   ⅛ teaspoon freshly ground black pepper
   1 tablespoon toasted pine nuts

Combine all the ingredients except the nuts in a bowl, and season with salt and pepper. Transfer to a serving bowl, and sprinkle with pine nuts.

Surprise Extras

The following additional recipes are contributed by Tom Valenti and appeared in *Dan's Papers*—a local rag that's a must-read for the seasonal resident. These recipes are for people who are on a maintenance level of their diet, so the carbohydrate counts are not included here.

Farm-Stand Tomato Bread Salad with Country-Grilled Chicken

Yield: 4 servings

Marinade for chicken:

   1½ cups macadamia nut oil
   ⅔ cup red wine vinegar
   1 clove garlic, minced
   ½ teaspoon chopped fresh thyme
   1 teaspoon fresh chopped rosemary leaves
   ⅓ cup grated parmesan cheese
   1½ teaspoon salt
   1 teaspoon fresh ground black pepper

   4 roaster chicken breasts—skin on, with ribs

In a mixing bowl, stir the marinade ingredients together well. Pour half the marinade over the chicken. Let it marinate at least ½ hour, turning once. While the chicken is marinating, prepare the tomato bread salad.

> 3 juicy, vine-ripened tomatoes, cut into 1-inch pieces
> salt
> pepper
> 3 thick slices of good quality sourdough bread, cut into 1-inch cubes and toasted
> ½ red onion, chopped into a fine dice

Lightly season the tomato with salt and pepper. Mix the tomato, bread, and onion in a bowl. Pour the remaining marinade over this mixture, and season to taste. Allow to marinate. Grill the chicken over medium heat, turning occasionally for 25 to 30 minutes or until firm to touch or juices run clear. To serve, divide the tomato salad evenly among four plates, and place the chicken on top.

Sagaponack Shrimp Succotash

Yield: 4 servings

> 24 shrimp (12–14 count), peeled, deveined, and butterflied
> ½ cup macadamia nut oil
> 1½ cup corn niblets but fresh from the cob, raw
> 1 bunch scallions, with most of green removed and the rest chopped fine
> Diced mushrooms, peppers, or other vegetable that's fresh and available at the stand
> ¼ cup white wine
> ⅓ cup chicken broth—low sodium
> 2 tablespoons butter

Heat the oil in a large sauté pan or a wok. Throw in the corn and scallions or other vegetables, and sauté for 1 to 2 minutes over high heat. Add the white wine, and cook off the alcohol for another minute. Add the chicken broth, and let come to boil for 30 seconds. Swirl in the butter for 30 seconds or until the butter is emulsified in the mixture. Then turn the flame to low, add shrimp, and allow to gently simmer in the mixture, cooking about 2 minutes on each side. Divide into 4 serving bowls, and serve with your favorite brown rice or other whole grain.

Peconic Grilled Fish with Herbed Maconnaise Served with a Cold Summer Salad

Yield: 4 servings

> four 6-ounce fillets of your favorite fresh fish
> 3 ribs celery, with the stringy, outer part removed, and cut thin at an angle
> 6 radishes, sliced into thin rounds
> 1 cup flat-leaf parsley (outer leaves only)
> 1 bulb fennel, sliced thin
> ½ red onion, sliced thin
> 2 tablespoons lemon juice
> 4 tablespoons macadamia nut oil, plus more for brushing

Put all salad ingredients in a stainless steel bowl, dress with 2 tablespoons lemon juice and 4 tablespoons oil, and add salt and pepper to taste. Mix well, and allow to marinate. Meanwhile, season the fish fillets with salt and pepper; brush them lightly with oil on both sides, then place the fillets on a hot grill and cook 5 to 6 minutes per side, depending on thickness and preferred degree of doneness. To serve, simply divide the marinated salad evenly among 4 serving plates, and place one portion of grilled fish atop each. Finish with a dollop of Maconnaise.

Maconnaise

Yield: 2 cups

> 3 egg yolks
> juice of ½ lemon
> 1⅓ cups of macadamia nut oil

Place the yolks and lemon juice in the bowl of a food processor. Turn the machine on, and slowly drizzle in the oil until the mixture is thick and emulsified. Season a portion of the Maconnaise with salt, pepper, and your favorite herb—tarragon, chives, basil, and so on. Another variation is to add as much caviar as you can afford or add Dijon mustard to taste. You will have a different recipe each time.

Maconnaise Variations

Because Maconnaise is so versatile and because the recipe makes quite a bit of Maconnaise, you can experiment with different flavors by adding to the basic recipe to create many variations and delicious dishes that are rich in monounsaturates. I always keep the basic Maconnaise in my refrigerator and use the following variations when I need a little change. They're all delicious, and you can easily make your own versions.

South of the Border:

Mix in 2 seeded and minced chipotle peppers in adobo sauce.

Asian:

Mix in 1½ teaspoons freshly grated ginger.

Steak Sauce:

Mix in 1 cup finely crumbled blue or gorgonzola cheese.

Dijonnaise:

Mix in 1 tablespoon Dijon mustard.

Japanese:

Mix in 1 teaspoon wasabi mustard.

Sunday Brunch:

Mix in 1 teaspoon horseradish.

Delhi:

Mix in 1 teaspoon each cumin and turmeric.

Provençal:

Mix in 1 shaving black truffle or 1 teaspoon white truffle oil.

Thai:

Mix in a chopped scallion, 2 tablespoons red chili paste, and 1 jalapeno pepper, seeded and chopped.

Main Beach Scallop Bake

Yield: 4 servings

24 ounces sea scallops
2 fresh tomatoes, seeded and cut into ¼-inch dice
1 dozen leaves fresh tarragon
1 tablespoon capers
2 tablespoons fresh parsley, chopped
2 tablespoons lemon juice, freshly squeezed
2 tablespoons white wine
3 tablespoons macadamia nut oil
fresh ground pepper
kosher salt

Grilled scallops are generally hard to handle unless skewered, so try this handy way. Take 20 inches of aluminum foil, place on a table, and create a lip all the way around the foil. Place the scallops on one half of the lipped foil. Mix all the other ingredients in a stainless steel bowl, and spoon over the scallops. Fold the remaining foil over the scallops, and firmly seal around the edges. This can be prepared 2 to 3 hours in advance, but no earlier. Preheat your grill, and if you have an upper shelf, place the foil package there; if not, directly over medium heat will do, close, and cook for 8 to 10 minutes—the scallops should still be translucent in the center. This can be served either immediately by cutting open the foil, being careful of the steam, and dividing equally onto 4 plates; or it can be served as a cold fish salad as well, simply by chilling overnight, depending on your weekend plans. If you prefer, this dish can also be baked in a preheated 375-degree F oven for 8 to 9 minutes.

East End Marinated Pork Tenderloin

Yield: 4 servings

> 4 small (6–8 ounce) pork tenderloins (total 1½ pounds)
> kosher salt
> freshly ground pepper
> 1 cup macadamia nut oil
> 1 tablespoon sesame seeds, toasted
> 1 teaspoon freshly grated ginger
> 3 tablespoons soy sauce
> 1½ tablespoons rice wine vinegar
> 1 teaspoon garlic, minced
> 14 ounces haricots verts

This should be prepared at least 2 hours in advance. Place the pork in an oven-proof dish. Lightly season each tenderloin with salt and pepper, and set aside. Combine the remaining ingredients except the haricots in a stainless steel bowl; stir well. Set aside 25 percent of the marinade for the vegetables. Pour the remaining marinade over the pork, and store in the refrigerator until ready to use, turning every ½ hour. When ready to grill, set the grill to high and remove the pork from the marinade. Cook for 5 to 6 minutes per side for medium rare, brushing the marinade over the pork as it cooks.

While the pork is marinating, blanch the haricots verts by placing in boiling salted water for 2 minutes. Remove from heat immediately, and put in ice bath to stop the cooking process. Pour the reserved 25 percent of the marinade over the beans, and refrigerate until ready to plate. When the pork is cooked, place one tenderloin on each plate, divide the green beans, and top with toasted sesame seeds.

Country Style Frittata
Yield: 4 servings

⅓ cup macadamia nut oil
½ Spanish onion, minced
1 green zucchini, cut into 1-inch cubes
1 yellow zucchini, cut into 1-inch cubes
1 dozen button mushrooms, quartered
10 eggs
½ cup water
2 tablespoons fresh chopped basil
salt
pepper
6 ounces goat cheese

Preheat the oven to 350 degrees F. Heat oil over medium heat in a large nonstick skillet; add the onion, and sauté for 2 minutes until tender. Add the zucchini and mushrooms, season lightly with salt and pepper, and sauté gently. Meanwhile, break the eggs into a bowl, and add the water. Beat until fluffy, then stir in the basil, and lightly season with salt and pepper. Pour the egg mixture over the vegetables, reduce the flame to low, crumble the goat cheese into pieces, and distribute evenly over the egg mixture. Transfer the frittata into the oven, and bake for 15 to 18 minutes or until the center is set. Jiggle the pan to make sure it's not sticking, and invert onto serving dish. Allow to cool slightly, and serve. This is also great as a lunch dish, served with a small green salad that's seasoned with macadamia nut oil, salt, pepper, and some freshly grated parmesan cheese.

APPENDIX A
RESOURCES

I'd like to mention a few individuals and companies in the food industry that you should know about. The resources in this book are not meant to be exhaustive but are places and products I feel comfortable suggesting.

To obtain MacNut oil, the best brand of premium Australian macadamia nut oil on the market, simply visit the Web site at www.macnutoil.com. You can find a list of places near you that sell the oil, or you can order it online and have it delivered directly to your door. I admire this oil so much that I helped form a company to make it readily available.

As I explained earlier, I want to introduce you to two chefs who made some of the recipes possible and who have helped to introduce New Yorkers and Hamptonites to the exciting and delicious flavor of Australian macadamia nut oil.

Tom Valenti is one of the most revered chefs in New York. His intensely flavored cooking has drawn raves from the food press for over a decade. He has been honored by every food major food critic and magazine in the country, including *Gourmet, Food and Wine, Bon Appetit, New York Magazine,* the *New York Times,* and many more. Tom is the author of *Welcome to My Kitchen* (HarperCollins) and *Soup, Stews, and One-Pot Meals* and is a frequent guest on the Food Network and most major television programs. Not only is Mr. Valenti a talented chef, he also has a heart of gold. He is the founder of Windows of Hope, which he started after the World Trade Center tragedy of 9/11 to help families of those in the food and beverage industry. He has raised over $20 million to date. For more information on Tom, kindly visit http://www.ouestny.com

Doug Rodriguez started his career in Miami and helped to introduce New Cuban cuisine to America. He has been recognized by the *New Yorker, Gourmet,* the *New York Times,* and the James Beard Foundation. Mr. Rodriguez is the author of *Nuevo Latino, Latin Ladles, Latin Flavors on the Grill,* and *The Great Ceviche Book.* He has made numerous television appearances, including *Late Night with David Letterman, Good Morning America,* the *Today* show, and *CBS Weekend This Morning.* For more information, please visit his Web site at http://www.chefdouglasrodriguez.com.

I think it's extremely important to eat as organically as possible, and that means finding organic meats. Most meats, even those marked *natural,* have come from animals that weren't fed properly. It's important to find meat from animals that eat what they're supposed to eat. When trying to decide about organic meats versus natural meats, the most important thing to keep in mind is that unless the animal was raised on foods it was genetically programmed to eat, its meat is not truly organic. A truly "organic" animal product would be a cow that was fed grass or a chicken that was fed natural prey like earthworms—things they would be eating if they were in the wild. Also, organically raised animals should have space to move about in and should not be caged. The ways in which animals are penned factor into the fatty acid content of their meat products.

Most natural animal products will be free of antibiotics and growth hormones. I say "most" because there is a governmental standard that allows farmers to call their meat "natural" if they feed their animals only a small percentage of antibiotics and growth hormones

Here is a list of some places where you can find true organic meats.

Beef

River Run Farm—503-728-4561

Western Grasslands—916-443-4319

New England Livestock Alliance—413-477-6200 or
   http://www.nelivestockalliance.org

Lamb

Jamison Farm—800-237-5262

Watson Farm—in Jamestown, Rhode Island

Pork

Porky Pine Hill—607-832-4574

Out of the Woods Farm—Hardwick, Massachusetts

Others include Dominion Farms, Rehoboth Ranch, Truth Hill Farm, and Windy Meadows.

Organic eggs from free-range hens can be generally found in most major supermarkets and specialty food shops. When buying fish, make sure it's not farm raised and that it isn't on the endangered species list.

I would like to mention some of the many low-carbohydrate vendors available around the country. Again, since there are so many of them, this isn't meant to be an exhaustive list but will serve as a guide to help you get started.

LowCarbSuccess—This company sells low-carbohydrate breads, pancakes, muffin mixes, and many other things. 512-759-2913 or http://www.lowcarbsuccess.org

Pure De-lite—This is primarily a chocolate company, but the chocolates are very good and are not made with sugar. 866-456-2272 or http://www.puredeliteproducts.com

Just the Cheese—This company makes great cheese snacks. 800-367-1711 or http://www.specialcheese.com

And, of course, if you want to contact me, you may do so via any of my Web sites: http://www.thehamptonsdiet.com; http://www.thinforgood.com; http://www.feedyourkidswell.com; and http://www.allergyandasthmacure.com. My mailing address is:

274 Madison Avenue, Suite 402
New York, NY 10016
212-779-2944
212-779-2941 (fax)

To make it easier for us to get the levels of monounsaturated fats that we need to stay healthy and decease our risk of cardiovascular disease, I intend to produce nutritional supplements using macadamia nut oil combined with the essential fatty acids GLA, EPA, and DHA. These supplements will meet strict requirements to satisfy your body's need for the correct fats. I will alert you about the availability of these supplements on my Web site, http://www.thehamptonsdiet.com.

Also go to my Web site also for information about my new line of low-carbohydrate, healthful food products for children. It has been one of my lifelong dreams to create products that kids will like—products that are good for them. I am hoping to have the first of these foods available by May 2004, so keep checking the Web site.

Monounsaturated fat is poised to take over the dairy market, too. Currently in Australia with almost a 5 percent share of the market, and soon to be in Canada, the United States, and Europe, is a milk that has no trans-fatty acids. Almost all of the saturated fat has been eliminated from this milk, and replaced with monounsaturated fat. The company that makes this milk also creates other monounsaturated-rich dairy products, including cheese and yogurt. The importance of a diet rich in monounsaturated fat such as the Hamptons Diet is only now starting to be fully understood as the technology is created to make the foods for this kind of diet available. I am very excited about these products. When they become available in the United States, I will post purchasing information on my Web site.

Supplement Companies

As promised, in this section I recommend supplement companies that, in my opinion, make superior products.

Contemporary Nutrition. This company prides itself on manufacturing uniquely blended products using well-researched and tested ingredients. Contemporary Nutrition is the sole distributor of Lean Mystique, a supplement perfectly suited for use with the Hamptons Diet. It is available online at http://www.CNIdirect.com/diet or by telephone, toll free, 1-800-820-7656.

Source Naturals. This cutting-edge company creates over 400 varieties of supplements, including vitamins, minerals, herbs, amino acids, and specialty nutraceuticals designed to address the root cause of imbalances by targeting multiple, interdependent body systems in a truly holistic approach. Notable Source Natural products include:

Gluco-Science: Supports healthful glucose and carbohydrate metabolism and helps regulate insulin sensitivity and uptake into cells

HeartScience: Addresses the complexity of heart disease from many angles, including homocysteine regulation, electrical rhythm, blood vessel integrity and energy generation

Inflama-Rest: Helps address the multiple causes of inflammation and the resulting underlying imbalance of the overabundance of pro-inflammatory omega-6 fats in our diet

L-Carnosine: Helps reduce glycation, a process in which DNA and protein are damaged by glucose; aids in lipid control; and is associated with positive antiaging benefits

Source Naturals products are available in health food stores worldwide; to find a store near you that sells these products or for more information, visit the company's Web site, http://www.sourcenaturals.com, or call, toll free, 1-800-815-2333.

Frequently Asked Questions of the Hamptons Diet

For the most part, you don't list portion sizes in the menus, why is that? When preparing the menus, I configured them in such a way so that the reader did not have to worry about determining portion sizes. I also thought that readers would begin to get the idea of portion sizes by following the recipes and, this way, form a new behavior.

Is this really a low-calorie diet disguised as a low-carbohydrate diet? No. The Hamptons Diet works by eliminating unhealthful foods that are your body does not metabolize well. When your body actively metabolizes food and increases its thermic effect, you can lose weight more quickly and efficiently.

Can I use the recipes from your other books on the Hamptons Diet? You most certainly can—just use macadamia nut oil in all the recipes.

If I am a competitive athlete, can I add more carbohydrates before an event? Absolutely. I would suggest at least doubling your amount of carbohydrates the day or two prior to the event to build up glycogen stores for your muscles.

Can fruit juice be substituted for fruit? Absolutely not. Fruit juice is a cleverly disguised form of sugar with no redeeming nutritional value. Fruit has fiber and pytochemicals that are healthy.

Can I continue to eat the way I have been but just substitute premium Australian macadamia nut oil for my other oil and lose weight? No. Unless you are already following a reduced-carbohydrate diet, you must cut out simple sugars and refined carbohydrates and follow the meal plans outlined in this book.

How can I use macadamia nut oil as a spread instead of butter? This is easy. All you have to do is mix a pound of softened organic butter with a cup of macadamia nut oil, blend until well mixed and place it in the refrigerator. It is delicious.

What can I take with me when I travel? Macadamia nuts, of course, or any type of nuts. Mixed vegetables, such as peppers, cucumbers, zucchini, also work. When in a pinch, you can always use a prepared low-carbohydrate shake or protein bar, but keep my cautions about these products in mind.

Can I pick my seven favorite menu days and just repeat them over and over? Of course you can, but this may lead to boredom, which is one of the most common excuses for stopping a diet program.

Can I take meals from one day and substitute them for another? You can do so as long as you stay within the recommended carbohydrate counts—just check the menu plans.

My physician says that low-carb is just a fad—how do I respond? Low-carb is here to stay because it is the healthiest way to eat. It has been shown to decrease cardiovascular disease risk factors, lower weight, decrease risk of diabetes, and with the addition of Australian macadamia nut oil and the emphasis on monounsaturated fat in the Hamptons Diet, low-carb has never been healthier.

More Tips for Healthful Eating

1. Never skip meals—this will make you hungrier and your metabolism will not function as efficiently as it needs to. Skipping meals is the most common cause of overeating and craving indulgence.
2. Always eat something before you drink any alcohol. People tend to get intoxicated more quickly when dieting, and drinking can lead to inappropriate snacking behavior.
3. Keep the big picture in mind. Always try to stick to your goal, which is to be healthier and lose weight. If you are committed to these goals, you will find it impossible to stray from them. Pretend your new program is as important as your career or your family. (It really is, by the way.)
4. Try vegetables as appetizers. Blanche (steam for 30 seconds or so) them and then dip into cream cheese, peanut butter, or sour cream.
5. Eat before going to a party or other social function. This is a concept known as defensive eating. If you do this, you will be less hungry later and less likely to partake of something you shouldn't.
6. Treat your dietary needs as if they were important. For small gatherings, call the hostess and ask what will be on the menu and if there is something that you can bring that will satisfy your dietary needs. Vegetarians do this all the time and no one gets offended. Your dietary requirements are just as important
7. Carry snacks with you. If you do this, you will never be caught in a situation where you will be without anything to eat.
8. Plan your eating day before you leave the house. During most days, we know where the day is going to take us. Plan where you are going to eat and if you are going someplace unfamiliar, take healthful food with you.
9. If you overeat or eat the wrong foods at one meal, do not let this carry over into the rest of your day and disrupt your eating regimen. It is a bump in the road; don't let it become a detour.

Start fresh at the very next meal. Starting the day incorrectly is not an excuse to spend the rest of the day or weekend on the same wrong foot.

10. Make better food choices. Choose nuts over chips or pretzels, diet soda (if you must) over regular, eat extra vegetables and salad instead of potatoes with dinner.

11. Set a small exercise goal for yourself each week. Try to stick to it, but don't think you are a failure if you don't keep to it. Be realistic in setting that small goal.

12. Reward yourself at the end of each successful week of dieting in ways that don't involve food: go to the movies, go bowling, buy a new CD, take a long bubble bath.

13. Drink water. Often when we think we are hungry, our bodies are actually thirsty.

APPENDIX B
THE PRODUCTION OF OIL

Once, in a conversation with a client named Jim, I explained how oils are refined and how they get to our table. Jim, a fifty-two-year-old gentleman, had told me, "This is the easiest diet I've ever been on." He lost seventy-five pounds in seven months and hadn't been this thin since college. He felt terrific, he'd quit taking diabetes and high blood pressure medications, and his cholesterol and triglyceride levels were better than they had ever been. He attributes all of this to his becoming monounsaturated-rich. Before our conversation, he had no idea that oils went through so much processing before they reached his table. He'd always thought that using olive oil exclusively was the right thing to do.

Jim said that the only reason he stuck to this diet and the only reason it worked for him was his exclusive use of Australian macadamia nut oil—a totally unprocessed oil.

For those of you who are interested in learning about the fascinating process of extracting oil, this appendix will help. *Fast Food Nation* did a great job of exposing that industry, and although I don't claim to be anywhere near as thorough as Eric Schlosser was, consider this a brief overview of how edible oils get to our table. It should further convince you of the benefits of Australian macadamia nut oil and of any other unprocessed or minimally processed food.

Stone Pressing

This is the traditional method of extracting oil from seeds and olives. It is still employed for certain very expensive olive oils. Stone pressing generates very little heat, thus the oil retains whatever natural antioxidants are present.

Hydraulic Pressing

This is traditionally used for avocados, some olives, and walnuts. In this type of pressing, the oil is squeezed from the ground-up food by means of a weight applied from above with the aid of a crank. This is the traditional way of extracting extra-virgin olive oil; however, just because it's traditional doesn't mean that's how it's done today.

Mechanical Pressing

This method is also known as expeller pressing and is basically the same as hydraulic pressing, except machines turn the cranks. However, because a machine turns the crank much more quickly than any human could, friction is created, and this produces heat—temperatures up to 190 degrees F. Because mechanical pressing is also known as cold-pressed, it's important to realize that the product is actually being heated in the processing. Since it takes more raw materials to generate an equivalent amount of product this way, it's rather expensive. To ensure that this is the only thing that happens to the oil you purchase, the label must read: "100% mechanically or expeller pressed." If it doesn't say that, then the next step occurs.

Solvent Extraction

This method was invented so that the residual pulp left over from the previous method could have the remaining oil removed, about 10 percent. During this process, the residual raw material is exposed to hexane, a volatile solvent that is considered carcinogenic and hazardous by the Environmental Protection Agency (EPA). The oil is then heated to around 230 degrees F, so that the hexane supposedly washes off. However, microscopic traces of hexane are still found in most commercial oils.

Mechanical/Solvent Extraction

This is the most common method used today and the main reason why olive oil prices are so low. The raw material is crushed at temperatures up to 230 degrees F. The oil is then squeezed out at an extremely high pressure, causing the oil to heat even more. During this process, the oil is exposed to light and oxygen, which can further break down its chemical structure, leading to enhanced free radical damage. Then a solvent, usually hexane, is introduced to the meal to get that last 10 percent or so of the oil. Any pesticide residue on the raw material will stick during the solvent procedure. The oil is next heated to remove the solvent, and this high temperature causes the weak bonds of a polyunsaturated fat to break apart (canola, safflower, sunflower, etc.), thereby creating even more free radicals. The natural antioxidant properties and natural preservatives of the oil are lost, and preservatives such as BHT and BHA have to be added—two substances that are suspected of causing cancer.

MacNut Oil Packing

This is a specialized mechanical extraction system, in which the oil is extracted in a no-oxygen, light-free environment. The expellers are kept at very low temperatures, around 70 degrees F, and the equipment is made from nonreactive metals such as stainless steel. This process keeps the fatty-acid content intact, does not destroy the natural antioxidants and preservatives, and decreases the chance of having free radical damage. No chemical solvents are used. The nuts are tested for pesticide residue by the Australian government, and there is none. The nuts are grown in Australia's ideal climatic conditions, are 100 percent expeller pressed under cold conditions, and are not chemically extracted, filtered, or bottled. The naturally occurring vitamin E, carotenes, chlorophyll, phytosterols, and phospholipids like lecithin can all be found in MacNut oil. The shelf life is five years, if kept in ideal conditions. MacNut oil has high levels of naturally occurring vitamin E, so it doesn't need added preservatives—unlike other oils, which usually have the chemicals BHT or BHA added to ensure that the oils last. Even other macadamia nut oils add vitamin E to prolong the shelf life. MacNut oil doesn't have to.

Another added benefit in the way MacNut oil is produced is that it's manufactured in a plant that processes only macadamia nuts. There is no risk of cross contamination for people who are peanut-sensitive. And best of all, that's the entire process. No other refining is done. In fact, MacNut oil can be considered an unrefined oil. It is simply crushed, filtered, and bottled. There is no degumming, deodorizing, bleaching, or anything else.

When I explain all this to my patients, they immediately want to go out and buy MacNut oil and throw their other oils away. I can't really blame them. Just ask Marjorie. She went from a size 26 to a size 14 dress in eight months on the Hamptons Diet. She had been on a different low-carbohydrate diet without experiencing much success when her girlfriend told her about my method. She liked the idea of eating good carbohydrates, because she couldn't imagine a life without any carbohydrates at all. She wanted to learn about good oils, too. She knew there was more to fat than just eating all of it that you wanted to. After switching to MacNut oil, she started to lose weight within a week and is now elated by her trim, monounsaturated-rich self.

The macadamia tree, known scientifically as *macadamia integrifolia,* is native to southeastern Queensland in Australia, where it grows in rain forests and close to streams. The macadamia was introduced in Hawaii in 1881, and then it was only used as an ornamental for reforestation. It wasn't until 1948, when several hybrid species were introduced, that the commercial macadamia nut industry began to thrive in Hawaii.

It is important to note that the Hawaiian species are man-made hybrids—the climate of Hawaii is not suitable for the original Australian macadamia nut species. With its warm nights, Hawaii never gets cool enough to produce the most ideal nut. However, the nuts grown in Hawaii are quite delicious. Having ideal climate, soil, rain, and sun conditions for growing macadamia plants to extract oil from is just as important as raising animals on their natural diets to produce organic meat. The same guidelines hold true for olive oils, too.

The edible part of the macadamia nut grows inside a very hard seed coat that is surrounded by a soft outer husk, which protects it from toxin residues, insects, and other pests.

The nuts of the Australian trees contain about 80 percent oil. The Hawaiian nuts have a more variable oil content, ranging from 65 to 75 percent. This difference is partially the result of the nuts in Hawaii having been cultivated as edible fancy nuts, whereas the Australian nuts are grown for their oil.

In addition to Australia, macadamia nut trees are grown for oil in New Zealand, Hawaii, South Africa, Kenya, Central America, and, in a limited amount, Southern California. A good tree at age ten will produce about fifty pounds of nuts each year. The harvested nuts have to be husked and spread in a cool, dry place, protected from the sun. Any contact with moisture, warm temperatures, or sunlight at this stage will result in damage to the fatty-acid quality of the nuts. They then have to be shelled, which is quite difficult to do because of the hardness of the seed coat.

As with any oil obtained from a vegetable source, macadamia nut oil contains no cholesterol. Even though macadamia nut oil does not have a high quantity of omega-3 fats, it does have the perfect 1:1 ratio that we are looking to achieve. If you do all your own cooking, using macadamia nut oil and taking a GLA supplement will give you all of the omega-6 fats that you need.

Besides having a perfect fatty-acid profile, macadamia nuts are high in certain vitamins, minerals, polyphenols, flavonoids, antioxidants, and other amino acids. Macadamia nuts are high in potassium so you don't have to eat bananas, a fruit with one of the highest sugar contents, as a source of potassium. Macadamia nuts are also high in magnesium, calcium, selenium, vitamin E, niacin, and folic acid, and contain smaller amounts of manganese, copper, and zinc. Other vitamins found naturally in the nuts in smaller quantities are pantothenic acid, riboflavin, and thiamine. As for amino acids, macadamia nuts are high in glutamine, leucine, tyrosine, and alanine. Glutamine protects the intestines and tyrosine is a precursor of serotonin, the "happy" brain chemical.

Marsha, a pop singer whom you have heard, came to see me with a secret—she was diabetic. She was petrified of gaining weight as she started to get older; she needed to get ready for the Grammy Awards and she wanted to look her best. She was taking medication to regulate her blood sugar, but she really wanted to stop taking it because it made her gain weight.

I put her on the Hamptons Diet, telling her to have her cook use MacNut oil to increase her levels of monounsaturated fats and started her on a fish oil supplement. She called the next day to ask incredulously if she could really eat everything I had recommended; she was used to dieting and starving herself. I emphasized that she should eat the foods on the plan I gave her and advised her not to miss a meal. Within six weeks, she had lost five pounds, not a lot of weight, but she didn't have much to lose. The better result was that her blood sugar levels were better than they had ever been. And, we reduced her need for medication by half. Today she no longer takes any medications and has great blood sugar readings—the best in her life.

MacNut Oil versus Macadamia Nut Oil

Glen, a famous writer (much more famous than me) and a Hamptons regular, came to me for help dropping twenty pounds that had accumulated over the winter months. Glen liked to hang out at the local watering holes, spending hours eating elaborate dinners prepared by some of the world's best chefs and lounging by the fireplace looking at the crashing waves—some less-than-energetic ways of enjoying the good life that the Hamptons has to offer, even in the winter. Although he often traveled to Palm Beach and St. Barth's in the winter, he much preferred being in cooler weather and staying closer to home with his horses. He was fifty years old and was an avid polo player in the summer, so I knew he could keep the weight off once it was gone. He gave me eight weeks, with a deadline of Memorial Day, to help him. Now, as any of you who diet know, I wasn't the one doing anything—it was all up to him.

I explained the Hamptons Diet secret—macadamia nut oil. He agreed to use the oil, stopped his other diet program, and made an appointment to see me in two weeks. By that time, he had lost only two pounds and was quite frustrated. Finally, he admitted that he was using another brand of macadamia nut oil. I told him that oils are not created equally. Using a quality oil is crucial in the Hamptons Diet and the money spent on the right oil will count as money well spent on your health. Glen bought a bottle of MacNut immediately and in the next two weeks he lost 8 pounds and by six weeks lost the entire twenty pounds he wanted to lose.

MacNut oil is 100 percent Australian macadamia nut oil, made from the finest nuts. It is delicious and luxurious, just as they prefer it in the Hamptons. And, my patients tell me it is no more expensive than a comparable grade of extra virgin, estate-bottled olive oil and is cheaper than most good extra virgin olive oils that aren't estate bottled. The Hamptons Diet emphasizes the importance of natural, wholesome foods, and MacNut oil is the gold standard of wholesome and natural, and is the only Australian macadamia nut oil I know of that is available in the United States. Just as you would prefer olive oil from Italy and champagne from France, you have to insist on macadamia nut oil from Australia.

Still More Processing

Once oils have been extracted, they have to be filtered to remove any particles before bottling or before they are subjected to further processing or refining. That leaves us with two more categories of oil.

Unrefined

These oils have high nutrient contents. MacNut oil is unrefined. Unrefined oils are known for being unstable and having short shelf lives. This is because once the bottle is opened, the fatty acids in the oil will combine with oxygen, causing the beginning of free radical formation. As a result, the oil turns rancid. Unrefined oils are not supposed to be used at temperatures higher than 320 degrees F because this heat can accelerate the free radical damage and the rancidity process. MacNut oil is an exception because it has large quantities of protective vitamin E, a potent antioxidant. Its smoke point can be as high as 410 degrees F. This means it can be used for frying up to that temperature and baking up to 450 degrees F before any free radicals form or rancidity occurs. Keep this cardinal rule in mind: The more processing an oil undergoes, the more nutritionally compromised it becomes—just like any other food product.

Refined

An oil is refined to remove the bioactive components. Thus, the color, the odor, the free fatty acids, and the flavor are essentially removed. The oil is first degummed by using citric acid to remove the lecithin, a phospholipid. It is then refined with a caustic soda, which accelerates the oxidation of the oil and creates soap. The oil is next bleached— that is, it's mixed with diatomaceous earth or clay to remove colors and odor. The temperature at which these processes occur increases during each step. We are now up to 230 degrees F. The oil is then deodorized, a process in which steam is blown through the oil under a high temperature of 470 degrees F. Oils that contain large amounts of waxes or stearines are winterized to reduce cloudiness. The oil is cooled to around 45 degrees F, these particles become solids, and the oil is then filtered. After that, BHT or BHA is added as a preservative. Some oils even have methyl silicone, a defoamer, added. Clearly, it's important to avoid any oil that has undergone these processes. When you buy canola oil, safflower oil, corn oil, most commercial oils that you probably now have in your cupboard, or any oil that is not 100 percent expeller pressed, this is what you're getting. Throw them away right now before you read any further, or they will surely kill you.

Hydrogenation: The Making of Trans-Fatty Acids

In this process, the polyunsaturates, which normally are liquid, are turned into solids at room temperature. Crisco is an example of this type of fat. The oils that are used in this process are generally the cheapest ones—soy, corn, and canola—which have themselves been damaged by the extraction process. They are then mixed with tiny metal particles, usually nickel oxide, and heated to a very high temperature. Next emulsifiers and starch are squeezed into the mixture to give it a better consistency, and it is steam cleaned to remove the unpleasant odor, then bleached. Artificial flavors and colors are added after that, and it is finally ready for the supermarket shelf.

During this heating process, the chemical structure changes; the result is a trans-fatty acid. This configuration allows the oils to be compactable, hence they can become solids. The process was originally invented in the late 1800s and came to the United States in 1909. Because butter melted on hot days and refrigeration wasn't readily available during that era, hydrogenation filled the need for an unmeltable shortening.

I have argued in this book that you should avoid using canola and most olive oils and the table on the following page shows why.

Most people think olive oil is the healthy oil choice and use it almost exclusively. I was in the same camp until I started to understand how oils affect health. You cannot use a cheap olive oil and expect to get a healthy product—it is just not possible. And, as far

	MacNut Oil	Canola Oil	Olive Oil
Monounsaturated Fat Level	85%	56%	70%
Saturated Fats	12%	6%	15%
Omega-6:Omega-3 Fatty-Acid Ratio	1:1	2.4:1	12:1
Smoke Point (in degrees F)	410	225–520, depending on level of refinement	325

as I am concerned, canola oil has no place in our food chain. The information I uncovered about olive oil and canola oil made my hair stand on end because, like most people, I believe most of what I read. I was fooled into believing olive oil and canola oil, the two most popular cooking oils in the world, were the ones to use.

Carrie, a sixty-four-year-old ex-debutante, current-style arbiter, and leading New York socialite with homes in Southhampton, Palm Beach, and a secluded Caribbean island, came to see me because she was exhausted all the time. Yes, it was summertime and the social scene was in full swing, but she just didn't have the drive to attend the Boys Harbor firework display or the Southhampton Hospital charity ball or any of the other events that attracted the paparazzi. She had always been a health nut and during our first visit when we discussed some of the basics, the conversation came around to cooking oils. She held up her hand and said, "Don't worry there, doc, I've got that under control. I only use olive oil when I am cooking and canola oil for salad dressings. I've been doing that for years." I explained the problems associated with both olive and canola oils and she was shocked, but happy, to make the switch because she really wanted to feel better.

Within two weeks, Carrie came back to the office reporting renewed vigor and not having to sleep as much. By the end of six weeks, she felt like her old self and had lost those troublesome ten pounds that she didn't think she would ever have gotten rid of at her age. She had also hastily organized and hosted one of the most talked about parties of the year at a secluded beach off Georgica Pond. She loved that the diet was so easy to follow, and she could not believe how delicious her meals had become since she had switched to using macadamia nut oil.

Olive Oil Facts

Olive oil varies in flavor, color, and aroma depending on the kind of olives used, the soil and climate in which the olives are grown, when they were picked, and method of pressing. All of these factors make a big difference in determining the health benefits of the olive oil.

There are some internationally recognized labeling guidelines, but not much else to regulate oil production. Spain is the largest producer of olive oil, but olive oil can come from many other countries, including Greece, Italy, Tunisia, Turkey, the United States, and elsewhere. Although Spain may be the largest producer, Italy is considered by the world market to produce the finest grade of olive oil.

Tuscany and Umbria produce greener, more fruity and pungent flavored oils because they are produced from olives that are still immature. Oils from Liguria, the Provence region of France, or Apulia have a golden hue, are sweeter, and have a nuttier flavor than other oils. These southern varieties are produced from ripe olives.

Olives are harvested at different times of the year, depending on the frost conditions of the growing region. In areas where there is no frost, olives are harvested in January or February; this is most common in the southern regions of Italy. In regions that get more frost, harvest time is in November and December. To ensure the highest quality of olives, they should be picked just before they ripen and milled that same day before the olives ferment, which usually starts within 3 to 4 hours after harvest. The best olive oils are made from olives that have been hand-picked or beaten from branches with sticks. It takes roughly 1,500 to 2,000 olives to make a quart of oil.

Olive oils are processed in a variety of different ways and the processing itself is crucial to creating a good oil. The creation of a superior olive oil is similar and more expensive than making a good wine. Wine can be manipulated during the fermentation process, but olive oil cannot. The flavor and texture of an olive oil come from the olives alone; the oil can be made to have a bland taste but adding flavor is not possible.

Losing Their Virginity

Virgin

To be labeled virgin olive oil, olives must only be pressed by a physical means, such as stone pressing or hydraulic pressing, under conditions that do not lead to physical decay of the oil. This oil cannot undergo the rest of the refining process and solvents may not be used in the process. The oil can undergo washing, decanting, centrifugation, and filtering. These steps give the oil a lighter flavor and texture and the oil that results is sometimes sold as "light" oil, having an acidity level greater than 1 percent but less than 2 percent.

Extra Virgin

This oil is made the same way as virgin olive oil. The only difference is the amount of acidity or free fatty acids that are present in the final product. Extra virgin has to have a less than 1 percent acidity level. The lower the acidity level, the better the product is.

Pure Olive Oil

Plain olive oil sometimes has the word *pure* on its label. This type of virgin olive oil doesn't have a quality flavor because of its high acidity level, and it must be blended with a better grade virgin oil to be palatable. This oil undergoes processing and its level of monounsaturated fat is variable, as are its color, aroma, and flavor depending on how much regular virgin oil the manufacturer blends with it.

Olive Pomace Oil

The restaurant industry usually uses this oil, which has a poor fatty acid profile because of its level of processing. This oil is derived from the part of the olive known as the pomace, which is left after the olive has been pressed or centrifuged. Solvents may be used to extract more oil from the pomace.

Light Olive Oil

Light olive oil is usually highly refined olive oil that has been steamed and bleached with peroxide to achieve a lighter color and flavor.

Acidity Levels

Extra virgin is distinguished from other grades of olive oil by its acidity level. The freshest olive oil made from unripe olives grown in cooler climates normally has a low acidity level, about 0.5 percent or less. The lower the acidity level, the higher the polyphenol and antioxidant concentrations will be.

An oil's free fatty acidity is a direct measure of the oil's quality and reflects the care taken from harvest to extraction to the sale and consumption of the oil. Measuring FFA (free fatty acidity) is a simple procedure performed on all edible oils. The degree of free fatty acids also affects an oil's smoke point. This is a reflection of how stable the oil is. The lower the free fatty acidity, the less damage has been done to the oil. Australian macadamia nut oil matches and surpasses olive oil in every aspect of its healthful characteristics. There really is no substitute for macadamia nut oil if you want to be monounsaturated-rich, lose weight, and get healthy with the Hamptons Diet.

Peroxides are the primary products of olive oil oxidation. The more rancid or oxidized the oil is, the more peroxides it contains. This is true of any edible oil and is a good measure of the healthfulness of an oil product. The maximum peroxide value of Australian macadamia nut oil is 2.0. The average peroxide value of olive oil is 3.5.

Olive Oil Mythology

Some manufacturers blend refined and virgin oils to achieve a better acidity level so they can label their product as extra virgin. Others send their product to Italy to be bottled so it can be labeled as a product of that country. As a result, a label that says extra virgin no longer distinguishes a quality oil from other oils. "Cold-pressed" is an obsolete term that is still used to sway consumers into considering an oil to be worth buying. There are minimal truth-in-labeling laws in the olive-oil industry.

Be aware that additives can be found in olive oil. An interesting additive that is inexpensive to manufacture is hazelnut oil. It is very similar to olive oil, making it the perfect additive for unethical manufacturers to include in olive oil. It is so similar that it is difficult to detect it even when analyzed by scientists. Canola and other cheap oils are sometimes added to olive oil, but these additives show up easier in chemically tested oils. Olive oil distributors inherently know what they are selling. I heard one dealer say, "The customers know from the lower price that I can't possibly be selling them 100% extra virgin olive oil, but they buy it anyway." So, don't buy a cheap olive oil if you choose to use olive oil.

If you want the most healthful extra virgin olive oil, look beyond the labels, and ignore the popularity of cold-pressed types of oil. To ensure that you are buying the highest quality olive oil that you can, simply look for the following attributes:

- acidity level: the lower the acidity level, the better the quality of the oil
- bottling date: use within a year of being bottled
- location: required to be on all bottled oil; the cooler the region, the healthier the oil

Can-ugly Oil

My pet name for canola oil is "can-ugly" oil. Since canola is a completely contrived substance, I thought it should have a ridiculous name.

Canola oil is derived from the rape seed, which is a member of the mustard family that also includes broccoli, kale, cabbage, and mustard greens. The modern methods for processing canola oil are what make it can ugly. The oil is removed from the seed by a combination of high-temperature mechanical pressing and solvent extraction. Then the oil is further refined, bleached, and degummed, each step requiring exposure to high temperatures and chemicals. Since unrefined rapeseed oil has a large amount of omega-3 fatty acids, the oil easily becomes rancid and foul smelling during these high-heat processes. As a result, the oil has to undergo another refining process, called deodorization, which removes a large percentage of the omega-3 fatty acids by turning them into trans-fats. This process is the cause of the high level of trans-fats generally found in canola oil.

The canola oil found on supermarket shelves has been refined, heated, and damaged beyond repair. Furthermore, the canola oil used in processed foods is hydrogenated and turned into harmful trans-fats, which, for all intents and purposes, render the oil inedible if not deadly. If you take away nothing else from this book, at least be aware of the dangers of using canola oil. I have to be as vocal as I can in encouraging people to avoid eating this damaging product. Even some of the most sophisticated health writers still report about this product as if it were healthful, while nothing could be further from the truth. Now you have the facts, which speak for themselves.

Yes, I want you to lose weight, but I want you to do so in a healthful way. This book shows you how to eat for the rest of your life. *The Hamptons Diet* is one of the first diet books to follow in the wake of the low-fat diet craze, written by someone who worked alongside the innovator of the low-carbohydrate diet, Dr. Robert Atkins. This book explores the scientific rationale behind the dangers of a low-fat diet and advises us where to go next in a cutting edge, Hamptons way.

I hope you have enjoyed this book and are now armed with the necessary information to get healthy and lose weight. I invite you to become rich—monounsaturated-rich—and thin!

RECIPE INDEX

GENERAL INDEX